Juanderful Leadership:

The Titanic Series –

Faith, Focus, and Strategy When the Ship Tilts

FOREWORD

In a world that often measures leadership by status and success, this book calls us back to a higher standard — one rooted in faith, humility, and purpose. *Juanderful Leadership* reminds us that true leadership mirrors Christ: compassionate, steady, and guided by conviction rather than control.

Faith is our foundation — *"the substance of things hoped for, the evidence of things not seen"* (Hebrews 11:1). Focus is where vision becomes action — *"Let your eyes look straight ahead... be steadfast in all your ways"* (Proverbs 4:25-27). Strategy is the bridge between intention and impact — *"The plans of the diligent lead surely to abundance"* (Proverbs 21:5).

This book will challenge, elevate, and equip you to lead with a heart anchored in God's wisdom. You will return to these pages again and again as you learn to choose character over comfort, vision over visibility, and purpose over pressure.

Prayerfully yours, Joanne Lightfoot Newby

Juanderful Leadership: The Titanic Series - Faith, Focus, and Strategy When the Ship Tilts

Published by Jackie Boatwright Publishing
An imprint of Juanderful Holdings LLC, Atlanta, Georgia, USA

This book is a work of inspiration and leadership development. The names, events, and reflections are drawn from the author's personal experiences, professional insights, and spiritual revelation. Any resemblance to actual persons, living or deceased, is coincidental and unintentional.

Printed in the United States of America ISBN: 979-8-218-84879-8

Library of Congress Control Number
2025924156

Cover Design: Jackie Boatwright Publishing.

Publisher: Jackie Boatwright Publishing.
For information, inquiries, or speaking
engagements:
jackie@juanderfulenterprises.com
www.jackieboatwright.com

Dedication

To my husband, **Dr. Kevin M. Daus**, my steady place in every storm.

Your wisdom, faith, and unwavering belief in me have been the anchor that steadied my ship through every season of building, breaking, and becoming.
You have covered me in prayer when I was weary, challenged me when I settled, and reminded me to keep steering when the waves rose higher than the dream.

Thank you for being both my calm and my compass; for seeing my strength even when I couldn't, for loving me through every evolution, and for standing beside me as we built this vision together.

Your leadership, grace, and partnership inspire me daily. This book is as much yours as it is mine because every chapter I write, I live with you by my side.

With all my love, always and forever,

Jacqueline

THE UNSHAKABLE LEADER

by Jackie Boatwright-Daus, Ed.S., MBA, BS
Founder of Juanderful Leadership

There's something sacred about storms. They don't just test what you've built — they expose what you've ignored.

Over the years, I've learned that leadership isn't about the spotlight — it's about the storm light. It's how you guide yourself and others when the noise rises, the ego whispers, and the world demands more than your soul can give.

This book, *Juanderful Leadership: The Titanic Series, Faith, Focus and Strategy When the Ship Tilts*, isn't about tragedy. It's about **truth**. The Titanic didn't just sink; it *taught*. It became a mirror for every leader who has ever ignored the warning signs, over-trusted their own strength, or underestimated the cost of pride.

I've led through failure, betrayal, burnout, and blessing. And what I know for sure is this: leadership that's not grounded in faith will eventually collapse under pressure. These pages are for those who want to rise differently, who want to lead with vision but stay anchored in grace.

⚓ Staying Grounded When Success, Ego, and Noise Rise Up

Success can be louder than failure, and sometimes, that's more dangerous. When things start working, when doors open and your name starts echoing, ego can slip in quietly dressed as confidence. You stop praying as much because it feels like everything's flowing. You stop listening because the applause drowns out the still, small voice that guided you there in the first place.

But ego is a thief in leadership; it steals gratitude, blurs clarity, and replaces vision with vanity. I've learned to check myself when life gets loud. Because if you don't stay grounded in humility, you'll start flying on pride, and pride always has an expiration date.

The higher you go, the deeper your roots must grow. Staying grounded doesn't mean thinking less of yourself; it means remembering Who got you there. Every opportunity is a platform for purpose, not a pedestal for ego.

When the noise rises, I return to stillness. When the spotlight shines, I bow my head. Because the moment you stop depending on God is the moment the ground starts shifting beneath you.

"The Titanic Didn't Sink Because of One Storm — It Sank Because Everyone Stopped Paying Attention."

Neglect always comes before disaster. The Titanic wasn't taken down by a single moment; it was the sum of many small ones. Warnings ignored. Corners cut. Confidence unchecked.

Leadership works the same way. We often fall not because of one catastrophic event, but because we stopped paying attention to the little things that hold everything together: integrity, awareness, empathy, and prayer.

Complacency is the silent killer of calling. When you stop checking the small leaks, when you start assuming you're "unsinkable," that's when pride quietly takes the wheel.

I've learned to listen to the subtle signs; fatigue that whispers, "you're doing too much," peace that starts to fade, relationships that feel forced. Those are the cracks forming below deck.

The Titanic didn't have to sink. And neither do we. The downfall comes when leaders mistake momentum for maintenance; when they chase expansion but neglect the foundation.

Greatness isn't built in grand gestures; it's preserved in daily discipline. Stay attentive. Stay humble. Stay aligned.

"Quiet Quitting in the Spirit"

We talk a lot about "quiet quitting" in workplaces; employees who show up physically but have checked out mentally. But there's another kind of quiet quitting we don't talk about enough, the kind that happens in the *spirit*.

It looks like praying less because you're tired. Serving without heart. Leading without listening. Showing up in body, but not in belief. You may still be working, but your worship has gone quiet.

I know that season: When you've been pouring out so long that you start running on fumes. You're exhausted, not evil. You're drained, not defeated. But if you don't refill your spirit, burnout will become bitterness.

Quiet quitting in the spirit happens when pain goes unprocessed: When disappointment numbs your devotion: When the weight of leadership outweighs your willingness to rest.

The solution isn't more work, it's more *Word*. It's more worship. More silence. More connection. It's finding your anchor again before the waves take you under.

God doesn't need your performance. He wants your presence. So, if you've quietly checked out, it's time to clock back in, not to your job, but to your *joy*.

Faith Over Feelings: Leadership Through Maturity

Feelings are real, but they're not reliable. If I led by how I felt, I would've quit a thousand times. Leadership demands emotional maturity, the kind that moves by faith, not frustration.

You can't always trust your feelings when you're in transition. Storms distort vision. Pain blurs perception. But faith remains steady even when your emotions are screaming for escape.

Mature leadership means showing up with consistency, not convenience. It means leading even when you're misunderstood, serving even when you're unappreciated, and staying the course even when you feel unseen.

Faith says, *"I'll trust You, God, even when I can't trace You."* It's walking forward when the map is blank, but the promise is sure.

As I've grown, I've learned that emotions make poor captains. They're waves; they rise and fall. Faith is the anchor that keeps you steady through it all.

You Can't Heal While Holding On

Healing and holding can't happen at the same time. To move forward, you must unclench your fists from what's behind you. You can't heal from what you keep rehearsing. You can't make peace with what you keep resurrecting. And you can't receive new blessings while clinging to old burdens.

For a long time, I tried to heal while still managing what broke me. I prayed for peace but kept answering calls from the chaos I was supposed to leave behind. God had to teach me that closure isn't His responsibility, it's my decision.

Letting go doesn't mean you don't care; it means you finally do. It means you care enough about your purpose to stop bleeding in the same place. It means you believe God enough to trust that what's gone wasn't meant to carry forward.

Healing starts when you release the past from your hands and let God take it from your heart. Because every time you loosen your grip, He fills your palms with grace.

The Calm Before the Climb

Every chapter that follows is a mirror; a reminder that leadership is less about control and more about character. It's not just about steering ships; it's about *surviving storms* with wisdom, grace, and unwavering faith. You can't avoid the waves. But you can learn to anchor differently. The Titanic isn't just a story of what was lost. It's a lesson on what must never be ignored again.

Stay anchored. Stay aware. Stay Juanderful.

Juanderful — pronounced *wonderful.*

A reminder that even when the ship tilts, the journey can still be beautiful.

CHAPTER ONE:

THE CALLING OF THE CAPTAIN

Before leadership becomes visible, it becomes personal. This first chapter is about calling—not position.

Before we begin this chapter, I want you to settle in. It's one you let sit with you because if you are leading anything or anyone, this chapter is going to name a weight you've already felt. This isn't a chapter you rush through.

"Everyone Can't Handle the Role"

Everyone wants the title until they feel the weight of it. Being "the captain" looks glamorous from the deck, until the storm hits, until the pressure mounts, until you realize that the safety of others depends on your steadiness.

Leadership isn't just a position. It's a *burden and a blessing* wrapped in responsibility. You don't get to clock out when things get hard. You don't get to disappear when people disappoint you. The captain doesn't abandon the ship, even when everyone else does.

That's why not everyone can handle the role. Because being a captain isn't about control, it's about calling. You can teach management, but you can't manufacture *mantles.*

There's a sacred weight that comes with leading; it's not just steering people, it's shepherding purpose. It's praying over decisions no one else understands. It's staying calm while others panic. It's seeing the iceberg coming and still having the faith to say, "We'll make it through."

The Titanic had a captain who was experienced, respected, and trained, but confidence without discernment is a dangerous combination. Leadership without humility leads to tragedy. Every captain must learn: the higher you rise, the heavier the accountability. So, before you crave the captain's chair, understand the cost. It's lonely sometimes. It's misunderstood often. And it requires obedience over opinion.

But when God calls you to lead, you can't hide in the crowd. You can't shrink because it's hard or hand off the wheel because it's heavy. When it's your calling, quitting isn't an option, because the assignment is bigger than your comfort.

And that's what separates captains from passengers. The passengers enjoy the journey. The captain carries it.

Captain's Note

There were times I didn't want the responsibility that came with leadership. Times I wanted to be the one sitting back, not the one steering. But God doesn't call the comfortable. He calls the committed.

The longer I lead, the more I realize leadership isn't something I chose. It's something I was chosen *for*. And that realization keeps me humble, grounded, and accountable for every decision I make. You can't fake calling. It carries a weight that training alone can't prepare you for.

Reflection

- Has leadership ever felt heavier than you expected?
- Do I see leadership as a role I earned or a calling I was entrusted with?
- Am I leading from ego, experience, or obedience?
- How do I handle the moments when leadership feels lonely or misunderstood?

Takeaway

Leadership is not an achievement; it's an assignment. And the title of "captain" isn't proof of power; it's evidence of trust.

Everyone can't handle the role because everyone isn't *called* to carry it. But if you've been chosen, lead with grace, with wisdom, and with faith. Because true captains don't chase calm seas, they answer the call to *command them.* ⚓

"The Weight of the Wheel"

Leadership That Costs Something. Taking the wheel looks easy until it's in your hands. From a distance, it seems simple; just steer and stay steady. But when you're the one responsible for direction, decisions, and every soul aboard, the wheel doesn't feel like wood and metal; it feels like *weight.*

Leadership has a gravity to it that most people never see. They see your outcomes, not your pressure. They see your titles, not your tears. They see your confidence, not your nights asking God if you're still the right one for the job.

The truth is, the wheel doesn't just steer the ship; it shapes the leader. Every decision you make becomes part of your discipline. Every mistake becomes a message. Every crisis becomes a classroom.

And the hardest part? You don't get to let go. Even when you're tired. Even when people complain about your course. Even when the same ones you're trying to save criticize the way you're steering. That's the cost of the wheel. The same responsibility that gives you authority also keeps you accountable. You can't afford to lead from emotion; you have to lead from *essence.*

The Titanic's wheel was manned by officers who followed orders, but leadership isn't just about obeying commands; it's about having the discernment to question direction when lives are on the line. Sometimes the real leader isn't the one at the top; it's the one who has the courage to speak when everyone else stays silent.

The weight of the wheel will test your character more than your competence. It will show you that being in charge doesn't mean being in control; it means being *entrusted.*

But here's the paradox: When you finally learn to surrender the outcome and just steer with obedience, the wheel feels lighter. Because leadership only feels unbearable when you think you're carrying it alone.

Captain's Note

I've held the wheel in seasons where I could barely see ahead; when everything in me wanted to stop steering and just let the current take over. But every time I did, God whispered, "Hold steady, I'm still the wind."

That reminder taught me something important: Leadership isn't about having all the answers; it's about staying faithful to the direction He gave you.

The wheel is heavy because it carries legacy, not just responsibility. You're not just steering a ship, you're shaping generations.

Reflection

- Where have I tried to control what I was only meant to guide?
- Am I steering with faith or with fear?
- Who's helping me hold the wheel when I get weary?
- How can I remind myself that I'm trusted, not trapped, by the calling?

Takeaway

The weight of the wheel isn't punishment, it's privilege. It means God trusts you with direction, even when others only trust you with results.

When leadership feels heavy, remember this: you weren't chosen because you were perfect; you were chosen because you could *carry it*. ⚓

"Navigating Through Nightfall"

When You Can't See the Way, Lead anyway. The Titanic didn't collide in a storm; it collided in the stillness of night. That's a leadership truth we don't talk about enough. Disasters rarely strike when everything feels chaotic. They happen when the world looks calm, quiet, and safe... when vision is limited and confidence is high.

Leadership in daylight is easy: when the waters are clear and direction is obvious. But *nightfall?* That's when your instincts are tested. That's when faith has to take the place of sight.

Every great leader will face a season of darkness; a time when the direction is unclear, the signals are faint, and the people around you start doubting whether you still know where you're going. But real leadership isn't proven in visibility, it's proven in *vision.*

When the light fades, your obedience becomes your compass. You learn to listen more than you look. You start trusting the voice of God over the voices of fear.

The officers aboard the Titanic saw darkness as safety. They thought calm waters meant clear passage. But stillness without awareness is deception. They ignored the warnings. They moved too fast for their visibility. They didn't crash because they were weak; they crashed because they were *unaware.*

That's what happens when leadership runs on momentum instead of mindfulness. You can't steer well when you're rushing. You can't hear God when you're noisy.

Navigating through nightfall means slowing down long enough to discern. It means leading from sensitivity, not speed. Because when you can't see the whole path, obedience becomes your map.

The night season will always test your posture. Will you panic, or will you pause? One keeps you frantic. The other keeps you faithful. Every dark season teaches you how to trust the unseen. And when daylight comes again, you realize it wasn't the darkness that almost destroyed you; it was your own fear of it.

Captain's Note

There were times I led in total darkness; no roadmap, no reassurance, just faith. And I learned that God does His best steering when you stop grabbing for the wheel.

Darkness isn't punishment; it's preparation. It trains your discernment. It sharpens your sensitivity. It forces you to depend on what's eternal instead of what's external.

When visibility is gone, lean in deeper. Sometimes God dims the light so you'll learn to *listen.*

Reflection

- What areas of my life or leadership feel dark or uncertain right now?
- Am I trying to force direction, or am I learning to trust divine timing?
- How do I respond when I can't see progress, with panic or patience?
- What has the dark season revealed about my faith, not my fear?

Takeaway

Nightfall doesn't mean you've lost direction; it means God is testing your navigation. You don't need to see the whole ocean to trust the Captain who made it. Leadership at night requires stillness, discernment, and courage. Because even when the path is hidden, the purpose isn't.

"The Lesson in the Hard Days"

When everything is easy, you don't pay attention. You start to assume the path will always stay clear, the people will always stay loyal, and the plan will always go as written. But life, leadership, and faith don't work that way, not if you're really growing.

The most valuable lessons I've ever learned didn't come from success. They came from struggle. The days that broke my rhythm taught me what structure really meant. The people who walked away taught me how to lead without applause. The closed doors taught me how to build my own.

"Calm seas" in leadership look like comfort, but comfort can dull your discernment. When everything runs smoothly, it's easy to think you're unshakable. But strength doesn't come from ease; it comes from endurance.

Growth happens on the days you don't want to show up but do anyway. It happens in the silence when no one's validating your effort. It happens when you decide to keep walking in purpose without an audience or an outcome.

The hard days refine your leadership lens. They teach you patience, humility, and how to read the room when energy shifts. They teach you to trust your gut when resources run low and voices get loud.

So, if this season feels hard, don't rush it. You're not being punished; you're being *prepared.* The calm doesn't teach you who you are; the challenge does.

And when the next season comes, you'll notice what used to shake you, doesn't; what used to offend you, can't; what used to break you, builds you now. Because calm seas don't make great captains, tough ones do.

Captain's Note

I used to think leadership meant control, keeping things smooth and predictable. Now I know leadership means composure, staying centered when nothing goes as planned.

The goal isn't to keep things calm; it's to stay calm. True leadership isn't proven when things are easy; it's proven when you can stand in chaos and not lose your character.

If this season is stretching you, it's not breaking you; it's *building your capacity.*

Reflection

- Where am I learning to stay steady even when the situation isn't?
- What kind of leader am I becoming when things don't go as planned?

- **How can I use what I've learned to** strengthen someone else?

Takeaway

The calm doesn't create competence; consistency does. *Every difficult moment adds weight to your wisdom. And one day, you'll realize you weren't learning how to manage storms; you were learning how to master yourself.* ⚓

"You Can Delegate but You Can't Abdicate."

There comes a moment in every leader's journey where you realize this: You can release tasks, but you can't release responsibility. Delegation is healthy: abdication is dangerous.

True leadership means knowing when to hand something off, but never handing away the direction, identity, or divine assignment of the vision. The Titanic didn't sink only because it hit an iceberg; it sank because too many people thought someone else was steering. Too many assumed "the next person" had the insight, the urgency, or the vigilance. At some point the vision was spoken, but it was no longer stewarded.

That is what happens when leaders get tired, overwhelmed, or surrounded by people whose commitment is shallow. It becomes tempting to step back and hope the team will "just get it." But vision doesn't grow in assumption, it grows in accountability. And God does not give *your* assignment to *their* hands.

You can train them.
You can trust them.
You can task them.

But you cannot transfer the mantle God placed on *you.* The weight of the calling rests where He originally put it. If you drop it, the vision drops with you.

On the Titanic, some roles could be delegated: passing out life vests, directing passengers, and sounding alarms. But there was only one captain responsible for the decisions that shaped destiny. A captain can instruct the crew but cannot surrender the wheel. A leader can share the work but must never surrender the watchtower.

Leadership requires presence. It demands clarity. It demands a voice that is steady even when the waters rise, when people panic, or when fatigue tricks you into silence. Because the moment you abdicate the vision, the ship begins to drift, and drifting always leads to danger.

So, stand up. Take the wheel back. Delegate the task but guard the vision. Because God didn't appoint you to simply announce where the ship is going. He appointed you to *ensure it gets there.*

Captain's Note

A leader's greatest responsibility is not doing the most work, it is protecting the direction. Others can carry pieces of the mission, but only you carry the calling. When the ship tilts, the team will look for your steadiness, your clarity, and your conviction. Never surrender the authority God entrusted to you.

Reflection

Question 1:
Where have you allowed fatigue, frustration, or fear

to make you step back from leading the vision God gave you?

Question 2:
What part of your vision needs you to take the wheel again, not with pressure, but with renewed authority and confidence?

Takeaway

Delegation is a strategy. Abdication is a surrender. You can share the work, but you can't hand away the vision. Your calling remains your responsibility, and your leadership remains the anchor.

"Before the Storm Breaks'

There is a moment in every leader's journey that rarely gets talked about: the moment before anything tilts, breaks, or rises. It's the space between the assignment and the adversity. Between the calling and the cost. Between knowing what God showed you and preparing for what it will require.

Most people assume leadership is defined in the loud moments, the crisis, the confrontation, the breakthrough. But seasoned captains know better. Leadership is shaped in the *quiet weight* of responsibility long before the waters swell. It's in the hours no one sees. The decisions no one praises. The discipline no one applauds. The conviction no one fully understands.

The Titanic didn't strike the iceberg because of one wrong move; it happened because somewhere along the way, people stopped respecting the still waters. They mistook calm for safety. Silence for security. Reputation for invincibility. And that's where many leaders fall apart.

The Titanic failed long before it struck ice. It failed in the calm, in the overconfidence, the noise, the distractions, and the belief that reputation could replace readiness. Your vision requires the opposite.

You must prepare inwardly before you elevate outwardly. You must sharpen your discernment before the waters demand it. You must know your role, own your calling, and steady your heart before the assignment asks more of you than comfort can carry.

This is where you assess your spiritual seaworthiness:

- Are you leading from clarity or convenience?
- Are you anchored or drifting?
- Have you allowed people, pressure, or noise to soften your grip on the mission?
- Have you tended to the cracks before they turn into catastrophic breaches?

Because storms don't expose the leader, they reveal the leader who failed to prepare. I write this as a reminder: Before the waters rise, reinforce the helm. Strengthen your faith. Secure your boundaries. Recenter your focus.

So, when the storm comes, and storms always come, you're not scrambling to find stability. You *are* stability. A leader who didn't just claim the vision... but prepared to carry it.

Trust me, before the storm ever arrives, God gives His leaders a moment, sometimes a short one, sometimes a stretched season, to steady their soul, strengthen their posture, and clarify what must not be compromised. Not because danger is present, but because destiny is near. This is the space where you learn:

- to listen deeper than applause
- to lead without needing agreement
- to prepare without needing validation
- to carry vision without dropping your identity

Leadership matures *before* the waters rise.
It is forged in the stewardship of the calm.
It is tested in the silence where God trains your instincts, your discernment, and your integrity.

By the time the waves finally come, true leaders aren't surprised. They're ready; not because the storm is easy, but because they refused to treat the stillness casually. And that is what separates captains from passengers.

Captain's Note

There comes a point in every leader's journey where God asks a quiet but life-altering question: *"Can I trust you with what's coming?"* Not the part you prayed for, but the part you didn't see; the pressure, the weight, the responsibility, the elevation that requires endurance more than excitement.

Before any great storm, heaven prepares the captain. And in my own life, the moments that stretched me the most weren't the crises themselves, it was the silence before them. The pause where God tightened my backbone, strengthened my discernment, and stripped away every illusion of control so that when the waters rose, my spirit did not.

The storm never creates your character, it reveals it. So, if God is preparing you right now, don't rush the process. Don't resent the stillness. Don't misinterpret the quiet as inactivity. Heaven does its deepest work before earth ever sees the shift.

This is the place where He sharpens your instincts, clarifies your vision, and strengthens your hands for the wheel. It's where He teaches you to lead from conviction, not convenience... from purpose, not pressure... from clarity, not noise.

And hear me clearly when God is fortifying you, it is never punishment. It is protection. Because when the waters rise, He doesn't want you scrambling to find your anchor. He wants you to become the anchor; steady, rooted, unshakeable, prepared.

Reflection

1. Where in your life have you been underestimating the stillness God gave you to prepare?
2. What habits, attitudes, or relationships need strengthening *before* your next level shows up?

Takeaway

The stillness before the storm isn't empty; it's essential. What you strengthen in silence becomes what you stand on in the waves. Honor the calm. Prepare with intention. Lead with readiness.

Captain's Notes

(Use this space to write freely.)

_____

_____

_____

_____

_____

_____

_____

_____

_____

_____

_____

_____

_____

_____

_____

_____

_____

_____

"You can share the work, but you cannot surrender the direction — the vision is safest in the hands God entrusted it to." — Jacqueline Boatwright-Daus

CHAPTER TWO:

WHEN THE WATERS RISE

If you're still with me, this next chapter is for you.

"The Storm Doesn't Mean You're Sinking"

I've learned to stop praying for calm seas. Because calm seas never taught me how to lead. Growth only happens when the waters rise. I didn't know the strength of my own anchor until life's currents started to pull me in every direction; until everything I thought I could depend on started to drift.

The storms I've faced didn't come to destroy me; they came to reveal me. They showed me what was rooted in faith and what was built on fear. They stripped away the false confidence I had in my own plans and the dependence I had on people who were never meant to hold my weight.

Anyone can look strong when the sun is shining, and the ship is still. But purpose and leadership, real, God-given leadership- are proven when visibility drops. It's in those moments when God whispers, *"Steer anyway."* And I'll be honest; I didn't always want to.

There were seasons when I wanted to drop the anchor and just let the tide take me wherever it wanted. But that's not faith. Faith isn't proven when everything makes sense; faith is proven when everything shakes. Every storm I've survived has exposed something in me, not to shame me, but to strengthen me. It forced me to remember who really holds the wind, who commands the waves, and who can still speak *"Peace, be still"* when I can't. So, when life feels like it's breaking apart, I don't panic anymore; I inspect my anchor. I ask myself: Is my faith rooted in feelings or in God? Is my purpose attached to applause or to obedience?

If my faith is real, it won't drift. If my purpose is in Him, it won't be lost. Because I finally understand, the storm never came to drown me. It came to define me.

Captain's Note

There was a time when I thought peace meant calm waters, but now I know peace means *trusting God even when the waves rise higher than your confidence.* Leadership will test every illusion of control you have. It will break you down to rebuild your foundation on something unshakable. I've learned that storms don't change your calling; they clarify it. Every time the wind hit harder, I became more certain that I was never steering alone.

Your Reflection Moment

Question 1:
What has God asked you to hold onto that looks like it's sinking right now?

Question 2:
Are you trusting the forecast, or the One who controls it?

"Faith Is Proven in the Flood"

Everybody wants faith until it's time to *use it.* It's easy to say, "I trust God," when the path is clear and the forecast looks calm. But true faith doesn't show up in the sunshine; it reveals itself in the storm. Faith is proven in the flood.

When the waters rise and the plan starts falling apart, that's when faith becomes more than a phrase; it becomes *a posture.* You can't fake endurance when the waves are crashing. You can't borrow belief when the ground beneath you gives way. Either you're anchored, or you're not.

There have been seasons in my life where everything that could go wrong, did. Dreams I was sure would flourish fell apart. People I trusted disappeared. The blueprint I built with prayer and strategy washed away overnight. And yet I kept hearing God whisper: *"Stay in the boat."*

At first, I didn't understand. Why stay in something that felt like it was sinking? But that's when I learned the difference between comfort and calling. Comfort jumps ship when the water hits the deck. Calling says, "I might be wet, but I'm not done."

See, the flood doesn't come to kill faith; it comes to prove it. The pressure reveals whether your belief was based on convenience or conviction. Anybody can praise when it's profitable. But when the storm hits, the applause stops, and the future looks uncertain, that's where the real believers are made.

Faith doesn't always look pretty. Sometimes it's swollen eyes, shaking hands, and whispered prayers that sound more like *"help"* than *"hallelujah."* But God honors that kind of faith. Because it's real. It's raw. And it's rooted in something deeper than outcome; it's rooted in obedience.

You don't need faith for what you can control. You need faith for what you *can't explain.* You need it when God says *build the ark* and there's not a cloud in the sky. You need it when everyone's watching you and wondering why you're still believing for something that looks impossible. And that's the beauty of the flood: it separates spectators from survivors. It washes away false support and reveals who's truly anchored.

If you're in a flood right now, don't curse it. It's not here to destroy your purpose; it's here to display your faith. Because when the water recedes, and you're still standing, everyone will know you didn't make it because of your strength. You made it because of your anchor. That's what Juanderful Leadership is built on, not calm waters but *tested faith.*

Captain's Note

I used to think floods were God's way of saying "I'm disappointed." Now I know they're His way of saying "I'm developing you." The greatest anointing in my life came after the moments I thought would break me. The deeper the flood, the stronger my anchor became. And every time the water rose, so did my awareness that I was never steering alone.

Your Reflection Moment

Question 1:
What current in your life right now feels like it's pulling you under? Is it possible that it's not punishment, but preparation?

Question 2:
What has the last storm revealed about your anchor, your faith, your patience, your dependence?

Action Step:
This week, write down one storm you've survived. Next to it, list the strengths that emerged from it. That's your proof; you're not breaking, you're being built.

Key Takeaway: *The storm didn't come to destroy you; it came to reveal what's anchored in you. Faith is proven in the flood, not the forecast.*

"Anchored, Not Afraid"

The ocean doesn't stop being powerful because the captain has faith; it's faith that steadies the captain *through* the power of the ocean. True leaders aren't fearless; they're anchored. They know storms are inevitable, but sinking isn't. To be anchored is to remain rooted in purpose even when everything around you shifts.

It's trusting God more than conditions, remembering that even if visibility fades, direction remains. Courage isn't about controlling the waves; it's about trusting the One who commands them. So, when the waters rise, you don't panic; you plant your feet, adjust your stance, and remind your crew: *"We may rock, but we won't roll under."* That's leadership through faith, not fear. That's being anchored, not afraid.

Courage isn't the absence of fear; it's the decision to stay anchored when fear comes. I've learned that being anchored doesn't mean the storm won't shake you; it means the storm can't separate you. Because faith doesn't erase the wind, it keeps you steady in it.

Every leader, every believer, every dreamer faces that moment when the waves rise higher than their confidence. You start wondering if you missed the mark, if maybe you sailed too far, too fast, or too faithfully. But here's what I've discovered: you can't lead in deep waters with shallow trust.

Being anchored means I've stopped asking God to calm every storm. Now I ask Him to strengthen my anchor. Because there's power in staying still when everything around you is screaming "move."

Fear whispers, *"You're not going to make it."* Faith replies, *"Even if I can't see the shore, I know Who holds the sea."* The storm doesn't scare me anymore because I've been here before. I've seen the waves rise, and I've seen them fall. And through it all, God never moved.

When your anchor is in Him, you don't have to control the tide; you just have to trust the tether. Anchored means grounded in grace, not glued by fear. Anchored means secure in calling, not shaken by circumstance. So no, I'm not fearless. I'm anchored. And that's better.

Captain's Note

I used to equate leadership with control: as if calmness proved competence. But now I know: the most effective leaders aren't the ones who avoid chaos; they're the ones who remain centered in it.

My peace doesn't come from everything going right; it comes from knowing God still reigns when everything goes wrong.

Your Reflection Moment

Question 1:
What do you rely on when everything starts to shake? Is your peace anchored in people or in purpose?

Question 2:
What truth about God steadies you when fear tries to take over?

Action Step:
Today, when anxiety rises, whisper to yourself, *"Anchored, not afraid."* Say it until your soul believes it.

Key Takeaway:

You can't control the wind, but you can choose where to drop your anchor.

"When the People Around You Don't Believe"

There's nothing heavier than carrying a God-given vision in an unbelieving environment. You can feel it, that quiet resistance when you start speaking about what God showed you.
Their silence is louder than words. Their doubt is subtle, dressed up as "realism" or "just being practical."

But what they don't understand is when God deposits a vision, He doesn't take a vote. He doesn't need consensus; He calls for obedience. And that means sometimes the people closest to you will have proximity but not perspective. They'll see you, but they won't *see it.*

When you walk with people who lack faith, your calling starts to feel like confusion. You start second-guessing the very thing God confirmed, not because He changed His mind, but because their unbelief diluted your confidence.

I've learned that unbelief is contagious, but so is faith. That's why protecting your environment is spiritual warfare. Because if you're surrounded by people who only believe what they can touch, they'll unintentionally talk you out of everything God is trying to birth through you. You'll hear things like:

"Maybe that's too big."
"You don't have the resources for that."
"Be realistic."

But here's the truth: faith was never realistic; it was obedient. It walks on water while logic looks for a bridge. It builds arks when there's no rain in the forecast. It plants seeds in famine because it trusts Who spoke, not what's seen.

So, when you find yourself surrounded by small vision, don't shrink yours. Shift your circle. Pray for alignment. Because the wrong company can make a God-sized assignment feel like a mistake.

And remember this, isolation in obedience is better than inclusion in disbelief. God will separate you before He elevates you. He'll pull you out from among the doubtful because what's inside you can't grow in contaminated soil.

So, if you've been walking alone lately, don't mistake that for abandonment; it's protection. God is preserving your focus for the fulfillment of the vision. And when it manifests, the same people who questioned your faith will witness your fruit. You're not crazy. You're just called. And sometimes, faith looks foolish until it's finished.

Captain's Note

There will come a point in your leadership journey when the people you thought would *see it* won't. Not because they're bad. Not because they don't care. But because God didn't give them the same view from the helm.

I had to learn this the hard way. There were seasons when I was steering by faith, but the people closest to me were measuring by facts. They couldn't see what I saw, and for a while, I tried to convince them. I tried to prove the vision, defend the assignment, and explain every divine instruction. But all that did was drain my focus and delay my obedience. Then God whispered: "You were called to lead, not convince."

That changed everything. Leaders often confuse validation with confirmation. But the truth is, belief is not always collective at the beginning. Noah built an ark with no audience. Abraham left home without a roadmap. Jesus led disciples who didn't fully believe until after the resurrection.

When people don't believe, it's not a sign you've missed God; it's a sign He's testing if you'll still follow when applause turns to silence.

You can't expect everyone to carry a revelation they didn't receive. Sometimes your obedience will offend comfort zones. Sometimes your growth will expose their stagnation. But your job is not to shrink the vision to fit their understanding, it's to stay faithful until they see what you've been building all along.

So don't take disbelief personally. Take it as proof that you're being stretched beyond human agreement into divine alignment.

Your Reflection Moment

Question 1:
When was the last time you paused your own progress, trying to convince others to believe in something God already confirmed?

Question 2:
How can you protect your vision in seasons where understanding is limited, and faith is your only fuel?

Action Step:
Take inventory of where you've been seeking validation instead of confirmation. Then pray: "God, teach me to stay focused even when I'm not fully understood. Strengthen my faith to keep building what You've shown me, even in silence."

Reflection

When those around you can't see what you see, remember faith is sight in seed form. Not everyone is meant to water what you've been called to plant.

The Titanic was a marvel of engineering, yet even brilliance couldn't prevent blindness. The crew believed in its unsinkability so much that they ignored the warning signs. In your life, disbelief works both ways. Some will doubt you too soon, others will believe too easily in the wrong things. That's why discernment matters more than validation.

God will often isolate your belief so He can solidify your trust. He'll let some voices fall silent so you can finally hear His. When belief around you wavers, anchor your focus in the One who called you. Your vision wasn't meant for public approval; it was meant for divine fulfillment.

Leadership Takeaway

The absence of belief around you is not the absence of purpose within you. You don't need everyone to understand your calling; you just need the courage to keep steering when they can't see the destination. Stay faithful. Stay focused. And remember, when they don't believe in you, believe in the God who does.

"Where I Was Called to Lead, Not Convince."

There comes a moment in leadership when you realize you were never called to convince people of your calling.

Convincing drains you. Leading develops you. And if you spend your strength trying to prove your purpose to people who don't even see theirs, you'll waste the very oil God gave you to pour into destiny.

For a long time, I mistook *influence* for *approval*. I believed that if I could just explain my vision clearly enough, if I could just talk long enough or love hard enough, people would understand what I saw. But you can't explain divine assignment to someone who's only tuned to convenience.

Some people aren't rejecting *you*; they're rejecting the stretch that your leadership requires. And if you're not careful, you'll start shrinking your message just to make room for their comfort. That's not leadership. That's compromise.

True leadership doesn't argue its anointing. It doesn't beg to be understood. It moves in quiet confidence, knowing that clarity comes through consistency, not convincing.

There's a difference between *pulling people along* and *walking in purpose.* The first makes you tired. The second makes you trusted. So now, I've learned to release the need to prove myself. If you see it, great, let's build. If you don't, may God open your eyes in His timing.

Because the moment I stopped trying to convince people, I finally had peace to lead people. And that's where the real fruit started to grow. Not in the debates, but in the direction. Not in the explanation, but in the execution.

Some won't follow until the vision manifests, and that's okay. Because when you're truly called, your results will do the convincing. Lead anyway. Lead with awareness. Lead without apology. You were never meant to *argue the assignment,* just *walk it out.*

Captain's Note

Leadership doesn't require everyone's agreement, just your obedience. You weren't chosen to convince; you were chosen to carry the call. Stop debating with doubt and start demonstrating with discipline. The noise around you will quiet once your results speak. Keep leading, even if no one claps.

Reflection

Question 1:

Are you leading to be understood or leading to be obedient?

Question 2:

What have you delayed because you're waiting for agreement from people who were never meant to understand the assignment?

Takeaway

When you stop convincing and start leading, peace replaces pressure. The faithful don't wait for validation — they move with vision. You were not called to gather approval — you were called to gather momentum. Lead boldly, quietly, and confidently. Your obedience will always prove what your explanations could not.

"When Vision Feels Like Conflict"

The most powerful lessons I learned in business weren't from books or conferences; they were born out of internal struggles and trying to help people whose vision was short.

I thought leadership meant helping everyone see what I saw. But what I learned is that some people aren't ready to see beyond the surface. When your vision stretches past someone's comfort, it doesn't look like inspiration to them; it looks like intimidation.

Every time I tried to push someone toward their potential, they felt I was pulling them away from their pride. Every correction became an accusation. Every redirection became *"you're talking down to me."* But the truth is, I wasn't talking down; I was lifting up. And that's when I realized something powerful: vision without maturity becomes offense.

Some people want leadership until it challenges their comfort. They want growth until it exposes their habits. They want opportunity, but not accountability.

What I learned through those seasons was this: Leadership isn't about convincing everyone to see what you see. It's about walking faithfully with those who *can*. It's about protecting your peace when your intention gets misinterpreted. And it's about knowing that not every disagreement is disrespect; sometimes it's just a reflection of someone's undeveloped discipline.

The hardest lesson? You can't mentor vision into someone who is comfortable being blind. And that's okay. Because your job isn't to drag people into destiny, it's to model it.

So now, I move differently. I no longer beg people to see. I lead with awareness, pray for discernment, and keep my heart soft, but my boundaries firm. Every argument taught me something about myself: Where I needed more patience. Where I needed to let go sooner. Where I was called to lead, not convince.

And that's how Juanderful Leadership was born from the tension between wanting to help everyone and learning that some people aren't ready for the deep end.

Captain's Note

There will be times when what God shows you makes people uncomfortable. Your vision will stretch others beyond what they can see, and sometimes, that stretching will look like tension. I've had seasons where every new idea seemed to offend the old system. Where every push for excellence was met with resistance. And for a while, I thought conflict meant I was doing something wrong until I realized, conflict is often the confirmation that growth has begun.

The Titanic didn't sink because of one mistake; it sank because the crew became too comfortable with the illusion of safety.
No one wanted to question the course, challenge the pace, or adjust the plan. The same thing happens in leadership when we silence conflict instead of studying it.

Vision doesn't destroy unity; complacency does. Healthy conflict refines teams, redefines priorities, and reawakens passion. It's when ego gets louder than mission that chaos takes the wheel.

So, when your vision starts stirring resistance, don't panic; pay attention. So many times, God uses friction to reveal who's truly aligned and who's just along for the ride.
Because where there's no resistance, there's usually no movement.

Reflection

Vision will always separate the committed from the comfortable. You can't lead people into a new season while allowing old patterns to dictate direction.

When your vision feels like conflict, it's not always because others oppose you; it's because they don't yet understand the magnitude of what's shifting. You're speaking future, and they're still living in the familiar.

Growth requires disruption. The ship doesn't turn without tension. And leadership requires courage, the courage to hold your course when misunderstanding feels like isolation.

Just like the Titanic's crew, many leaders ignore subtle warning signs because peace feels safer than truth. But ignoring conflict doesn't preserve peace; it delays disaster. The maturity of a leader is tested not when everything runs smoothly, but when everything shakes and you still choose to steer.

Your Reflection Moment

Question 1:
Have you been mistaking necessary tension for disloyalty, when it may actually be growth calling you to refine your leadership approach?

Question 2:
What vision have you silenced to keep the peace, and how has that silence delayed your progress?

Action Step:
This week, instead of avoiding conflict, lean into understanding. Ask God: "Show me what this resistance is revealing, not what it's ruining." "Give me the grace to confront with wisdom and the courage to lead with love." Then, write down three areas where your vision has been challenged, and beside each one, note what that conflict is teaching you about your next level.

Leadership Takeaway

Vision will always cause friction before it creates focus. The same waves that rock the ship are often the ones that carry it forward. Don't retreat when conflict comes — refine your course, secure your crew, and keep steering toward destiny.

"Leading Through Uncertainty"

The longer I lead, the more I realize leadership isn't tested in moments of clarity; it's revealed in moments of chaos. It's easy to look composed when everything is predictable. But when the unexpected hits, when plans crumble, people shift, or pressure mounts, *that's* when grace has to take the wheel.

Grace under pressure isn't pretending you're fine. It's remembering Who holds you when nothing else feels stable. It's the quiet strength that keeps you from reacting out of fear or frustration. It's learning how to breathe when everyone else is panicking.

There were times in business when I felt cornered by the weight of leadership. Deadlines stacked, emotions clashed, and people I thought I could depend on suddenly disappeared. My old self would have snapped. My new self, the one God was building, stayed still.

Because grace doesn't deny reality. It invites God into it. Grace says, *"I don't know how this is going to work out, but I trust that it will."* Grace allows you to speak peace into a room without pretending the fire isn't burning. Grace lets you handle pressure with poise instead of panic.

Uncertainty doesn't destroy strong leaders; it develops them. You only learn to lead in the fog by walking through it. You only discover peace under pressure by surrendering control. Every uncertain season has been my classroom, and every collapse has been my certification. Now, when uncertainty comes, I don't question God's presence; I assume His preparation. Because the same pressure that tried to break me also taught me balance.

Grace under pressure doesn't mean I never cry, doubt, or stumble. It means I refuse to stay there. It means I lead from a calm spirit when my emotions want to revolt. It means I respond with wisdom when worry begs for reaction. And most of all, it means I've learned the art of resting while responsible. Pressure might test my patience, but grace will always protect my posture.

"Knowing When to Row and When to Bail"

Every leader eventually faces a moment when the ship starts taking on water, when the plan that once felt unsinkable suddenly starts to tilt. And in those moments, your survival depends not on how strong you are, but on how well you discern your role.

Some storms call for oars, to row, to push forward, to persevere through resistance. Others call for buckets, to bail water, to stabilize what's left, to protect what still floats. The difference between the two is divine wisdom.

Many leaders lose themselves because they confuse the two. They keep rowing when they should be bailing. They're so determined to reach the destination that they ignore the damage beneath their feet. They exhaust their team pushing forward when God has already whispered, *"Pause, protect, and repair."*

The Titanic was built for speed, not stillness, and that became its downfall. The obsession with progress blinded leadership to prudence. The captain and crew were so focused on moving forward that they ignored the signs telling them to slow down. Leadership isn't just about momentum; it's about management knowing when forward motion is no longer safe.

In life and business, "rowing" represents action, drive, and ambition, the push toward success. "Bailing" represents stewardship, wisdom, and sustainability, the humility to preserve what's important before chasing what's next.

The most dangerous thing a leader can do is row a sinking ship. You can't steer vision from a vessel that's already flooded with neglect, pride, or exhaustion. Some seasons require movement; others require maintenance. The wisdom to know the difference will determine whether your mission survives the storm.

When God gives you a vision, He also gives you rhythm, a divine pace that protects your purpose. But when you force progress without alignment, you start taking on water. Pride rows harder; wisdom pauses and bails.

Rowing without discernment creates burnout. Bailing without faith breeds fear. But when you allow both to exist in balance, rowing when called, bailing when necessary, you lead with maturity, not panic.

The fact of the matter is, storms don't just test your strength; they test your judgment. Sometimes the greatest act of leadership isn't pressing forward but *preserving what remains.*

Captain's Note

I learned that success isn't always about acceleration; sometimes it's about preservation. There were seasons when I was rowing with everything I had, wondering why the progress felt heavy. I didn't realize I was rowing a ship full of leaks.

Then God reminded me: "You can't row and bail at the same time." He wasn't asking me to quit: He was asking me to shift. To patch what was broken before pushing forward again.

Every vision requires seasons of repair. Every storm reveals what's weak. The wise captain doesn't see the pause as punishment; she sees it as preparation.

Reflection

- Am I rowing when this season requires me to stabilize instead?
- Have I mistaken movement for progress?
- What areas of my vision are taking on water because I've ignored the signs to slow down?
- How can I rebuild rhythm between progress and preservation?

Takeaway

Great leaders don't just chase momentum; they manage moments. You can't steer effectively if your vessel is sinking under stress, imbalance, or misalignment. Row when it's time to advance. Bail when it's time to preserve. And never confuse stillness with stagnation; sometimes God stops your oars to save your ship.

Because every captain must learn: *Speed will get you there, but wisdom will keep you there.* ⚓

"When Vision Requires You to Step into the Unknown"

Faith will always demand movement before evidence. It doesn't wait for calm seas or perfect conditions; it walks straight into the waves believing that God's voice is stronger than the storm.

Every great leader reaches a "Peter moment" that season when God calls you to do something that defies logic, breaks routine, and tests trust. You've spent years learning to navigate the ship, but now He's asking you to *walk on water.*

That's when leadership transforms from strategy to surrender: When you can't rely on titles, talent, or timelines, only trust.

Peter didn't walk on water because he was extraordinary; he walked because he recognized the voice calling him. His obedience, not his ability, kept him afloat. In leadership, it's the same; the miracle isn't in the walking; it's in the *willingness to step out.*

Most people never experience supernatural outcomes because they stay in the safety of the boat. The boat represents what's familiar, your comfort zone, your old system, your last success. But at some point, leadership requires leaving what's predictable for what's *possible.*

You'll never see new outcomes holding onto old anchors. Faith in leadership means walking toward the calling, even when the conditions contradict the promise.

When Peter began to sink, it wasn't because the water changed; it was because his focus did. Distraction drowns faster than doubt. And in leadership, where your eyes go, your faith follows.

Leaders don't fail when storms come; they fail when they forget who called them into the storm in the first place. If God called you to it, He factored in the waves. He accounted for the fear, the risk, the nights you'd want to go back to the boat. But He also planned for your *resilience* the moment you'd rise again, soaked but stronger, humbled but whole. Leadership is not walking in perfection; it's walking in faith, even when your feet tremble.

Captain's Note

I've learned that faith in leadership is rarely comfortable. You can't lead people through storms you're too afraid to walk through yourself. But the miracle always meets movement.

When you step out, even uncertain, even unqualified: Heaven steadies what's beneath you. God doesn't need you to have all the answers; He just needs you to keep your eyes on Him. So, if He's calling you out of the boat, don't argue, *walk.* The waves will recognize the voice that sent you.

Reflection

- Where is God asking me to step out in faith, even when it doesn't make sense?
- What "boats" (comfort zones, fears, systems) am I being asked to leave behind?
- How can I keep my eyes on the promise instead of the pressure?
- What miracle might be waiting on the other side of my obedience?

Takeaway

Leadership by faith isn't about being fearless; it's about being focused. You may stumble, you may sink, but as long as your gaze stays upward, your purpose will never drown.

Faith doesn't eliminate the storm; it teaches you how to walk through it. Because great leaders don't just survive the water — they walk on it.

"Keeping Your Spirit Above the Storm"

Leadership will always come with weight; the weight of vision, responsibility, and people who depend on your direction. But even the strongest captains must remember faith is the only thing that floats when everything else starts to sink.

The danger in leadership is learning to carry so much that you forget how to breathe. You begin to equate exhaustion with excellence, thinking that the more you do, the more you prove your worth. But faith doesn't work that way. Faith doesn't ask you to carry the ocean; it asks you to trust the One who walks on it.

The Titanic didn't sink because of the water around it; it sank because of what got *inside.* In the same way, leaders don't drown because of the pressure outside; they drown because they let it in.

When you let stress, comparison, or self-doubt breach your spirit, your buoyancy of faith weakens. The goal isn't to avoid deep waters; it's to protect your belief while you're in them.

Faith that floats doesn't deny the weight; it decides what's worth carrying. It means learning to release what isn't yours to hold. You can't lead effectively if you're overloaded emotionally, spiritually, or mentally. You must travel light to rise high.

Sometimes God doesn't calm the storm because He's teaching you how to stay above it. He's showing you that the same water that drowned others will hold you up if you keep your faith intact.

So, when leadership feels heavy, take inventory of what's filling your ship. Unrealistic expectations? Let them go. Unnecessary battles? Drift past them. Unspoken fears? Release them.

Because when you strip down to faith, you float again. And the most powerful leader is the one who learns that *surrender doesn't sink you; it saves you.*

Captain's Note

Faith doesn't remove the weight; it redefines how you carry it. There were seasons when I tried to hold everything together: people, plans, and pressure, and I nearly drowned under my own expectations.

Then I learned: I was never asked to hold it all. I was only asked to believe. The moment I released the need to control outcomes; peace began to carry me again. The water didn't get shallower — my faith got stronger.

Reflection

- What responsibilities or burdens have I been carrying that God never assigned me?
- Have I allowed external pressure to become internal panic?
- Where in my leadership do I need to trade performance for peace?
- What would it look like to lead lighter, anchored in faith, not fear?

Takeaway

Faith isn't fragile; it's buoyant.
Even when the storm rages, faith knows how to rise.
The secret to spiritual endurance isn't learning to fight the water; it's learning to float in it.
Because when you stop resisting and start trusting, your faith becomes your life jacket. ⚓

Captain's Chapter Reflection: When the Waters Rise

Faith Over Fear in the Midst of the Storm

Before you move forward, take a moment to breathe. When the waters rise, leadership isn't about steering faster; it's about standing firmer.
This is your pause between the crash and the calm, your space to anchor, listen, and learn from the waves.

Captain's Reflection Prompts

1. **When my "ship" began to tilt, what was my first reaction — faith or fear?**
   What did that moment reveal about my trust in God's timing?
2. **What warning signs did I ignore because I was too focused on moving forward?**
   How can I respond differently next time?
3. **How do I define peace in the middle of uncertainty?**
   Is my peace based on progress, or on presence?
4. **What people, habits, or thoughts cause unnecessary waves in my leadership?**
   What can I release to restore calm?
5. **What is this storm teaching me about myself as a leader and as a believer?**

Captain's Notes

(Use this space to write freely.)

_____
_____
_____
_____
_____
_____
_____
_____
_____
_____
_____
_____
_____
_____
_____
_____
_____
_____
_____
_____
_____
_____

"Faith isn't proven by calm seas — it's revealed by
the courage to stay when the waters rise."
— *Jacqueline Boatwright-Daus*

CHAPTER THREE

THE RIGHT TEAM

*If what you just read resonates, the next chapter
goes deeper."*

"The Power of Stillness in a Shifting Sea"

There comes a point in every leader's journey when motion becomes noise. You've rowed until your arms ache, bailed until your strength fades, and yet the waves keep coming. That's when discernment whispers; *drop the anchor.*

Anchoring doesn't mean giving up; it means grounding yourself when everything around you is unstable. It's the decision to stop reacting and start remembering who's in control of the waters.

Too often, we mistake movement for progress and activity for productivity. We think the louder we row, the faster we'll reach the shore. But the truth is, storms aren't always meant to be outrun; some are meant to be *waited out.*

The Titanic didn't pause when the warnings came. The captain trusted the vessel more than the voice of caution. Leadership failure doesn't always look like chaos; sometimes it looks like *confidence in the wrong thing.* When you ignore divine instruction to rest, you drift from alignment into assumption.

Dropping the anchor is an act of surrender, not weakness. It's the leader's way of saying, *"God, I've done all I can in my strength; now steady me in Yours."* Anchoring is where humility and hope meet, where the leader stops trying to control the tide and learns to trust the timing.

In leadership, there are seasons to row, seasons to bail, and seasons to anchor. The problem is, most of us only know how to do the first. We love momentum because it feels like purpose. But sometimes, Heaven is teaching us that maturity looks like restraint, staying grounded while the waves rage.

Anchoring means letting the storm pass without capsizing your peace. It's sitting in the stillness long enough to hear what God is trying to teach before He moves you again. The same God who sent you into the deep will send calm to the sea in His time, not yours.

Captain's Note

There was a time I thought stillness was a setback; that if I wasn't moving, I was missing out. But I learned that anchoring isn't the absence of progress; it's the preparation for it.

Every captain needs a moment when God says, "Be still and know." Anchors aren't meant to keep you stuck; they're meant to keep you *steady.*

When you drop the anchor, you're saying: *"I trust Your direction more than my own momentum."* Because what's rooted doesn't drift.

Reflection

- Where in my life or leadership have, I mistaken stillness for stagnation?
- Have I been so focused on progress that I've ignored peace?
- What is God trying to teach me in this season of pause?
- Am I anchored in purpose, or am I drifting in pressure?

Takeaway

The sea doesn't scare those who know how to anchor. Storms don't destroy what's grounded in faith — they simply reveal what isn't. Before you chase what's next, secure what's now. The anchor is your reminder: you can pause without quitting, rest without retreating, and trust without proof. Because real leadership isn't about racing the waves — it's about remaining when they rise. ⚓

"When Peace Feels Like Isolation"

Sometimes God quiets the storm around you not to punish you, but to prepare you for the next one. You prayed for peace. You asked God to remove the distractions, the chaos, the constant pressure of keeping everything together, and when He did, the silence felt almost unbearable.

You thought peace would look like celebration, but it showed up as separation. The truth is, peace doesn't always come with applause; sometimes it comes with absence.

There's a kind of peace that feels lonely, not because you've lost your way, but because God has cleared the deck so you can finally *see* the way. When everyone else drifts away and the noise dies down, it's not punishment. It's positioning.

I remember the season when everything got quiet for me, the calls stopped, the doors slowed, and people I once leaned on began to fade into the background. At first, I felt rejected. Then I realized, God wasn't rejecting me; He was reintroducing me to me.

Peace will do that. It strips you of performance. It detaches you from dependency. It silences everything that used to define you, until all that's left is truth.

That's when you start hearing the voice that's been guiding you all along, the one that doesn't need validation to confirm direction.

Just like the Titanic's final moments, calm water can be deceptive. The night was still, but danger was beneath the surface. That's why peace without presence can be perilous; if you don't discern the season, you'll confuse calm for comfort instead of calling.

So, when peace feels like isolation, don't panic, lean in. This is the moment when God whispers your next assignment. This is where vision gets refined and endurance gets restored. Because before God releases you into your next season, He'll always test if you can handle peace without panic.

It's easy to lead when there's noise, motion, and validation. But can you still lead when it's just you, God, and silence? True peace isn't the absence of storms; it's the maturity to stand still even when there aren't any.

Captain's Note

When God quieted my world, I thought something was wrong. Everything that once made me feel "productive" slowed down: calls, projects, and people. I kept trying to reignite momentum, but every door I pushed stayed shut.

Then the Holy Spirit said, "This silence is not punishment. It's surgery." That hit me. I wasn't being benched; I was being *built.* Peace was never the problem; my dependency on motion was.

In leadership, we often define worth by how much we're doing. But real power isn't in movement, it's in mastery. Peace is where mastery is born.

Now, when things get quiet, I don't rush to fill the silence. I sit. I listen. I strengthen. Because peace is not the end of purpose, it's the foundation for the next wave of it.

Reflection

Peace has two sides: stillness and solitude. One heals you, the other reveals you. When peace feels isolating, it's not because you're being left behind; it's because God is removing the crowd so you can hear *clearly.*

The Titanic's still waters teach us something: silence doesn't always mean safety. You can't rely on the calm to define direction. You must rely on conviction. So, when God quiets your surroundings, don't question your calling; refine it. Stillness is where strength matures.

Your Reflection Moment

Question 1:
Have you been resisting God's peace because it doesn't look like progress?

Question 2:
What distractions have you been trying to resurrect in order to avoid feeling alone, when isolation may actually be God's instruction?

Action Step:
This week, sit with the silence. Journal what you feel God is teaching you about rest, renewal, and readiness. Pray: "God, teach me to rest without running. Show me that peace is not punishment, but preparation."

Leadership Takeaway

When peace feels like isolation, remember, silence is not God's absence. It's His invitation to rebuild your strength, realign your spirit, and rediscover your stillness.

"The Right Team"

No ship, no matter how powerful, can sail without a capable crew. The same is true in leadership. The strength of your vision is only as stable as the people who help carry it. Having the right team means surrounding yourself with individuals who don't just share your goals; they share your *values.*

True alignment isn't about numbers; it's about nature. It's not how many people you have, but who they are when the pressure rises. The right team doesn't just celebrate your wins; they protect your focus. They see the iceberg before you do and aren't afraid to sound the alarm. They understand that loyalty isn't silence; it's stewardship.

The Titanic had a state-of-the-art design, but not everyone aboard shared the same vigilance. Some trusted the ship's reputation more than the captain's warnings. Others were distracted by luxury and position. And a few ignored the red flags altogether. Leadership failure doesn't begin with incompetence; it begins with imbalance.

A team that lacks alignment will always leak energy, no matter how skilled the individuals are. Skills may fill positions, but unity fills purpose. A mismatched crew can make even the strongest vision unstable. That's why great leaders don't just *select* people; they *discern* them.

The right team complements your weaknesses, protects your blind spots, and moves in rhythm with your purpose. They don't compete with the captain; they cooperate with the course. You can teach skills, but you can't train integrity. You can assign roles, but you can't manufacture heart.

When the right people are in place, your mission doesn't depend on constant motivation; it moves on shared conviction. Because real teams don't just work together; they *believe together.*

When you're leading something significant, who stands beside you matters just as much as what stands before you. The wrong team can make a divine vision feel like a daily drain. The right team, however, multiplies momentum.

Discernment is your greatest tool in building teams. Never confuse enthusiasm for endurance, or availability for alignment. Everyone looks ready when the water's calm, but storms reveal who's truly called.

The Titanic's tragedy reminds us: credentials don't equal character. Some people can navigate charts but can't handle crisis. Others can follow instructions but lack conviction. The right team needs both competence and character.

As a leader, your responsibility is to identify not only who fits the *job* but who honors the *journey.* The right people don't just execute orders;

they embody excellence. They understand that loyalty isn't blind obedience; it's shared accountability. And when the storm comes (and it always does), you'll see who's rowing, who's watching, and who's quietly drilling holes in the boat. The right team won't just keep you afloat, they'll help you sail farther than you ever could alone.

Captain's Note

I've led teams that looked strong on paper but weak in purpose. Early in my leadership journey, I mistook talent for trustworthiness and availability for anointing. I kept people on the ship who were comfortable, not committed, and it cost me peace.

God had to teach me that not everyone who starts with you is meant to stay with you. Some are seasonal, not foundational. Others are assigned to observe, not to build.

Now, before I add anyone to the team, I pray for *alignment over assignment.* I ask, "God, send those who are called to carry this, not just benefit from it." Because when your team is right, your load feels lighter. And when your crew is wrong, even calm waters feel like a storm.

Choose wisely: not just who can help you, but who can *hold you accountable* to the vision when you're weary. The right team doesn't just guard the dream — they guard *you*.

Your Reflection Moment

Question 1:
Who on your current team reflects your vision, and who just repeats it?

Question 2:
Are you surrounding yourself with people who challenge you toward purpose or comfort you into complacency?

Action Step:
Take a moment to evaluate your circle.
Pray this: "God, align my team with my vision. Remove what drains the mission and strengthen what sustains it. Help me discern who's meant to row beside me in this season." Then make one intentional leadership adjustment this week, even a small one, to strengthen your alignment.

Key Takeaway:

The right team doesn't just move with your vision; they multiply it. Choose people who share your values, not just your goals, and your ship will always stay steady in the storm.

"When Obedience Feels Unrewarded"

Sometimes obedience doesn't produce results; it produces refinement. There's a part of leadership no one warns you about, the quiet space between obedience and outcome.
That place where you've done everything God told you to do, but the results look nothing like the promise.

You gave your yes. You followed the instructions. You stayed faithful, and yet... nothing seems to move. The doors haven't opened. The people didn't stay. The numbers don't show growth. And you start wondering, *"Did I miss something?"*

But here's the truth: obedience doesn't always show fruit immediately; sometimes it first exposes roots. When God calls you to something big, He often allows you to walk through a season that tests not your ability, but your *trust.* He'll give you an assignment that looks unrewarded in the natural but is building strength in the spiritual.

I've had seasons where obedience didn't bring applause; it brought isolation. It didn't open doors, it closed them. It didn't increase; it refined. But when I looked back, I realized every "unrewarded" act of obedience was shaping my leadership in ways results never could.

The Titanic reminds us of this truth. The engineers obeyed the design, but leadership overlooked the details. Even perfect execution can fail under pride and impatience. Obedience doesn't guarantee control of outcomes; it guarantees alignment with purpose.

God doesn't measure success by what you achieve; He measures it by what you *obey.* Some of your greatest blessings are delayed, not because you did something wrong, but because the reward you're waiting for is still being built.

Obedience that feels unrewarded is not wasted; it's being recorded. Every act of faith you think went unnoticed has been seen, counted, and stored by the One who rewards in His own timing.

Sometimes, God delays visible reward, so you won't confuse gratitude with gratification. He wants you mature enough to keep leading, sowing, and believing, even when it feels like nothing's growing. Because true leadership isn't proven by applause; it's proven by endurance.

Captain's Note

I've been in seasons where I questioned everything. I followed every instruction, stayed in position, led with integrity, and still, nothing seemed to move.

I remember saying to God, *"Why would You call me here just to let it all fall apart?"* And He replied, "I didn't call you to see results. I called you to reveal faith." That changed my entire outlook.

Obedience isn't about immediate reward; it's about *internal realignment.* It's about trusting that even when the stage is empty, heaven is applauding.

Leaders often mistake obedience as a formula for success. But obedience is not about outcome; it's about order. God's order always comes before His overflow.

Now, when I don't see results, I remind myself: "The silence doesn't mean I'm off course, it means heaven is still building the reward."

Reflection

Obedience will stretch your faith in ways favor never will. When everything you do seems unseen, that's where character grows. That's where your "why" gets purified.

The Titanic's downfall was not a lack of action; it was misplaced confidence. They obeyed what they understood but ignored what they didn't want to hear. That's the danger of conditional obedience following when it's convenient but quitting when it's quiet.

God doesn't reward partial obedience; He rewards faithfulness through silence. Even when no one claps, keep building. Even when no one notices, keep steering. Because in the kingdom, unseen obedience is never wasted effort; it's a sacred investment.

Your Reflection Moment

Question 1:
Have you been measuring your obedience by visible results instead of internal peace?

Question 2:
What area of your leadership is being tested right now, and could this "quiet season" actually be proof that you're in divine alignment, not delay?

Action Step:
Take inventory of where you've grown through obedience, not reward. Journal one moment where you followed God's direction even when it didn't make sense, and note what that season built in you.

Then pray: "God, teach me to trust Your process even when I can't see progress. Strengthen my faith to lead through silence until the reward reveals itself."

Leadership Takeaway

When obedience feels unrewarded, remember silence doesn't mean absence. Heaven pays close attention to faithfulness, even when the world doesn't applaud it. Keep steering, Captain. The reward is already on the route; you're just being refined to carry it.

"Assignment Vs. Alignment"

Every person connected to your mission has an *assignment*, but not everyone is in *alignment.* The difference between the two can determine whether your organization thrives or quietly drifts off course.

An assignment is about a *task;* it's what someone is hired, called, or positioned to do. But alignment is about a *heart posture;* it's whether that person's purpose, attitude, and belief system move in harmony with the greater vision.

On the Titanic, every crew member had an assignment: navigators, engineers, stewards, musicians, but not all shared the same awareness or urgency. Some worked the job; others guarded the mission. When the ship began to sink, the difference became clear. Those in alignment stayed committed to service until the end. Those only in assignment, looked for a way out.

In leadership, you can have a team full of skill and still lack synergy. Alignment creates unity that no title, contract, or paycheck can produce. People in assignment complete tasks; people in alignment *carry the vision.*

The aligned don't need constant motivation because their drive comes from conviction, not compensation. They understand *why* they're here, not just *what* they're doing.

That's why great leaders must discern who's present for the *position* versus who's present for the *purpose.* Assignments build function, alignment builds foundation. And when both connect, that's where excellence and endurance meet.

So never confuse participation with partnership. Some are assigned to the *moment*; others are aligned with the *mission.* Your job as a leader is to know the difference and lead with enough wisdom to keep your ship filled with those who see not just what they do, but why they do it.

A leader's greatest mistake is assuming presence equals participation and productivity equals passion. Assignments fill roles, but alignment fills gaps. People can fulfill their duties and still not share your heartbeat.

Alignment is what keeps a team steady when storms come. When hearts beat together in rhythm with the mission, obstacles can't divide them. But when the team is filled only with assignments, commitment becomes conditional; they'll row only as long as the water's calm.

When I walk into any organization or room I lead, I can sense it; the difference between people who *work for me* and those who *walk with me.* The first group asks, "What do I need to do?" The second asks, "How can I help it grow?"

Alignment creates ownership. It inspires accountability that supervision could never force. And when your crew is aligned, you don't have to micromanage the mission; it moves naturally.

Captain's Note

I've led enough teams to know this truth: gifted doesn't always mean *graced* for the journey. Some people join because they see the glory, not the grind. Others come because they love the idea of leadership, not the reality of labor.

God had to teach me how to separate *assignment energy* from *alignment spirit.* Assignments look impressive; alignment feels anointed. The aligned don't just understand the vision; they protect it. They pray over it, speak life into it, and correct anyone who mishandles it.

There was a time I kept people in position out of loyalty, even when they were no longer in alignment. It cost me peace, progress, and purpose. Now, I choose differently. I don't just ask, *"Can they do the work?"* I ask, *"Can they carry the weight?"* Because when the waters rise, skill helps you survive, but alignment helps you *sail.*

Your Reflection Moment

Question 1:
Who in your circle is in assignment and who is truly in alignment?

Question 2:
What systems or habits can you implement to keep your team aligned with the vision's core values?

Action Step:
Take inventory of your crew this week.
Write down your key players and ask God to reveal where alignment is strong and where it's slipping. Pray this: "God, show me the difference between who's assigned to my journey and who's aligned with my journey.

Key Takeaway

Alignment is greater than assignment.
Not everyone walking with you is meant to build with you. True progress happens when you surround yourself with people who share your vision, values, and spiritual foundation, not just your proximity or your plans.

"Protecting The Vision"

Every great leader must learn that the vision isn't just something you *build,* it's something you must *protect.* Vision is fragile in its infancy and sacred in its maturity. It carries the weight of your calling, the blueprint of your obedience, and the fingerprints of God's intent for your life.

But like a ship setting sail, vision is most vulnerable not to storms but to sabotage, distractions, disloyalty, and the subtle erosion of focus.

Protecting the vision means guarding the atmosphere around it. Not everyone who celebrates your idea is equipped to carry it. Some will applaud the dream but dilute the discipline. Others will agree with your goals but resist your growth. A true visionary learns to listen beyond words to discern who's adding wind to your sails and who's quietly cutting your ropes.

When the Titanic launched, it was magnificent, grand, admired, and unmatched. Yet pride in its perfection blinded leadership to the very details that could have preserved it. In the same way, when your vision starts succeeding, your greatest threat isn't the storm, it's *complacency.*

To protect the vision, you must:

- **Set boundaries.** Vision weakens when everyone has access to it.
- **Stay prayerful.** The enemy doesn't attack what isn't a threat.
- **Guard your culture.** What grows in your team's spirit will shape your results.
- **Keep clarity sacred.** If you don't define the vision daily, confusion will redefine it for you.

Protecting the vision isn't paranoia, it's stewardship. It's saying, *"This dream costs too much to be handled carelessly."* Because once you stop guarding what God gave you, the world will start reshaping it into something smaller, safer, and less sacred.

Leaders don't just cast vision; they *cover* it. They ensure the mission remains pure, the message remains clear, and the momentum stays anointed. Because when vision is protected, even in storms, the ship doesn't lose direction; it simply learns how to navigate deeper waters.

Captain's Note

There was a season when I shared the vision too freely, hoping everyone would see what I saw and feel what I felt. But I learned that not everyone who's *connected* is *committed,* and not everyone who's *present* is *purposed.*

God had to teach me that the vision isn't public property; it's a sacred assignment. There were times I gave access to people who admired the dream but weren't anointed to develop it. And each time, I was reminded that vision must be guarded, not just given.

I used to think protecting the vision meant being secretive; now I know it means being *spirit-led*. I cover the vision in prayer before I cover it in plans. I no longer pray only for expansion; I pray for *protection*. Because I've learned: what's not covered will be corrupted, and what's not guarded will eventually drift.

As a leader, I carry this truth: close vision is holy ground, and only those who honor it should walk on it.

Your Reflection Moment

Question 1:
Who currently has access to your vision that might not be assigned to it?

Question 2:
What distractions or influences have been quietly diluting your focus?

Action Step:
Take one evening this week to pray over your vision. Ask God to: "Expose what endangers it, reveal who's meant to protect it, and strengthen me to defend it with grace."

Then write down three protective measures you'll put in place, boundaries, habits, or people, to safeguard your next level.

Key Takeaway

Vision without protection becomes vulnerability. Guard what God gave you with prayer, discernment, and discipline because not everyone who can see your vision is meant to steer it.

Captain's Reflection: The Right Team

Knowing Who's Rowing with You and Who's Drilling Holes

Every great vision requires great people but not everyone aboard your ship is meant to steer. As a leader, it's your responsibility to discern who's aligned with your purpose and who's simply along for the ride. This reflection is your pause to evaluate loyalty, alignment, and leadership stewardship.

Reflection Prompts

1. **Who in my circle is truly rowing in rhythm with the vision and who may be resisting the current?**
   What fruit reveals their heart?
2. **Have I confused talent with trustworthiness?**
   How can I prioritize integrity over skill?
3. **Who covers the vision when I'm not in the room?**
   What does that reveal about alignment versus assignment?
4. **What boundaries or communication structures can strengthen my crew?**
   Leadership unity starts with clarity.
5. **If my mission faced a storm today, who would help me steer and who would abandon ship?**

Captain's Notes

(Use this space to write freely.)

_____
_____
_____
_____
_____
_____
_____
_____
_____
_____
_____
_____
_____
_____
_____
_____
_____
_____
_____
_____
_____
_____

"The right team doesn't just row; they guard the
vision when the waves rise."
— _Jacqueline Boatwright-Daus_

CHAPTER FOUR

THE POWER OF LETTING GO

As we continue, this next chapter focuses on release.

"Divine Completion and Releasing Control"

One of the hardest things I've ever had to learn as a leader and as a woman of faith is how to recognize when something is divinely complete.

Completion doesn't always look like closure. Sometimes God ends things quietly. No warning, no farewell, no grand explanation, just a stillness where movement used to be. And if you're not spiritually aware, you'll mistake that stillness for failure. You'll keep trying to revive what Heaven already retired.

There's a deep difference between something being *broken* and something being *finished.* Broken things can be mended. Finished things must be released.

For years, I tried to control outcomes God had already called complete. I'd pour energy into projects, partnerships, and people who had already served their purpose in my life. I didn't realize that my attachment to how things "used to be" was blocking the new things waiting to unfold.

But divine completion requires discernment, the ability to sense when grace has lifted from a season. When your spirit no longer feels the same alignment. When peace no longer accompanies the plan. That's not the enemy working against you. That's God signaling transition.

And here's the truth: releasing control isn't a sign of weakness, it's an act of worship. It's saying, *"God, I trust You more than I trust my own timing."* Because every time I've tried to hold on to what was finished, I ended up exhausted and anxious. But every time I've surrendered what I didn't understand, I found peace that didn't make sense.

There's power in being able to say, *"This season served its purpose."* There's freedom in closing the book without resentment, knowing the chapter completed what it was designed to teach you.

So now, when something shifts, when people drift or doors close, I no longer panic. I pause. I ask, *"Is this breaking me, or completing me?"* Because not every ending is a loss. Some are divine promotions in disguise. Completion isn't punishment. It's God saying, *"You've graduated. Let's go higher."*

Captain's Note

I used to think letting go meant losing control. Now I understand it's how I *gain peace.* Leadership taught me how to build. Faith taught me how to release. And together they've taught me that obedience is better than attachment.

Every time I've refused to let go, I delayed what God was trying to deliver. But the moment I released control, what I'd been praying for had room to arrive. Letting go isn't the end of leadership; it's the maturity of it.

Your Reflection Moment

Question 1:
Where in your life have you been trying to hold together what God already called complete?

Question 2:
What would peace feel like if you trusted that endings are divine direction, not rejection?

Action Step:
Today, write down one area where you're still gripping control. Say this out loud:

"God, I release what's finished so I can receive what's next." Then breathe. That's surrender, and that's strength.

Key Takeaway:

Completion is not loss; it's graduation. Release control and make room for what's divinely next.

"Everyone Who Starts with You Isn't Meant to Finish with You"

When God gives you a vision, it's natural to want to bring everyone you love on the journey. You want the people who clapped for you in the beginning to still be there when you cross the finish line. But the truth is not everyone who starts with you is meant to finish with you.

Some people are assignment-based, not lifetime-based. They were sent to help build the foundation, not dwell in the structure.
And when that season ends, trying to hold on to what's meant to move will always cost you peace.

At first, I took it personally. When people walked away or relationships shifted, I saw it as rejection. But over time, I learned that divine separation is a form of spiritual protection.
God knows who can handle your next level, and sometimes, the only way to elevate you is to prune your circle. Not every absence is betrayal.
Some are deliverance. And you'll know it's divine when their departure brings peace instead of bitterness.

The hardest part of leadership isn't managing others; it's managing your expectations of them. You can love someone deeply and still have to release them gracefully. You can be grateful for their role and still know their chapter is closed.

Because here's what I've learned: The vision God gave you wasn't a group project. It was a personal assignment. Some people were never supposed to carry the weight of what was placed in your spirit.

And when you try to drag them into a destiny they weren't designed for, you don't just slow them down, you sabotage yourself. They'll grow resentful. You'll grow weary. And what was once divine alignment becomes emotional entanglement.

It takes maturity to bless someone's exit without bitterness. It takes discernment to say, *"This connection served its purpose."* And it takes faith to keep moving forward when the crew changes mid-journey.

The Titanic didn't just sink because of the iceberg; it sank because too many people believed the wrong ones were meant to stay aboard.

When I say this, I am pointing to a deeper truth about misplaced loyalty, poor discernment, and leadership blindness.

The iceberg was only the visible cause; the external event that everyone remembers. But beneath that, there were human decisions rooted in ego, illusion, and favoritism.

Leadership on board the Titanic prioritized status over strategy. Many lifeboats were launched half empty because those in charge believed that only certain people, the wealthy, the prominent, the "important," deserved a place in them.

In a leadership sense, this means: Sometimes, the downfall of an organization, a team, or even a vision isn't caused by the obvious external challenge, it's caused by who you kept aboard when God was telling you to release them.

Leaders sink when they keep the wrong people close out of guilt, comfort, or sentiment instead of discernment. When you believe everyone is meant to go with you, you'll overload your ship with wrong assignments and drain your resources keeping them afloat.

The Titanic was unsinkable in design, but fragile in decision-making. The leaders trusted the wrong voices, ignored the right warnings, and gave authority to people guided by position instead of purpose. In context, this becomes a leadership warning:

You can have the strongest vision, the best systems, and the clearest direction but if you don't discern who belongs aboard for this leg of the journey, you'll risk sinking a divine mission by trying to save everyone.

Now, I move differently. I don't chase who drifts or beg who leaves. I trust that the same God who started this journey with me will send the right people for the next stretch. I've learned to honor those who helped build the ship, but not to anchor to anyone who was only meant to sail for a season.

Captain's Note

It used to break my heart when people I loved no longer aligned with my direction. But one day, God showed me, *you can't expect lifelong loyalty from temporary assignments.*

Some people were there to teach, some to test, and some to transition you. Now, when relationships shift, I don't question my worth, I check God's timing. And every time I release what He's completed, I rise a little lighter, a little wiser, and a lot freer.

Your Reflection Moment

Question 1:
Who in your life may have already completed their purpose, but you're still trying to hold on to them out of fear or comfort?

Question 2:
What has God been trying to end that you've been trying to extend?

Action Step:
Write down one relationship, role, or partnership that feels heavy instead of healthy.
Pray this prayer:

"God, if it's complete, give me peace to release it. If it's still mine, give me grace to carry it." Then trust His answer.

Key Takeaway:

Everyone who starts with you isn't meant to finish with you. Learn to bless the exit as much as you celebrated the entrance.

"Some Seasons are Completed"

Not everything that ends is a loss.
Some things have simply fulfilled their purpose. But
because we've tied our identity to the assignment,
the friendship, or the title, we mistake *completion*
for *collapse.* We start asking, "What did I do
wrong?" when the better question is, "What did this
teach me?" God isn't always closing doors to
punish you; sometimes He's protecting your destiny
from getting trapped in yesterday's grace.

Every season comes with a spiritual
expiration date. The favor that once fueled you
can't always follow you. The fruit that once fed you
eventually ripens, and if you cling to it too long, it
spoils in your hands. There's a danger in idolizing
what was meant to be temporary.
When we glorify what God already called
complete, we delay what He's trying to *continue.*

I've learned to see endings differently now.
When a season shifts, when the doors I used to walk
through suddenly close, when the people I leaned
on drift away, when the rhythm I built no longer
feels aligned, I don't panic. I pause. I listen.
Because endings are God's way of whispering,
*"You've learned enough here. It's time to grow
there."*

It takes discernment to recognize divine
completion. The moment grace lifts, peace follows.
What once flowed starts to feel forced. What once

inspired you starts to drain you. And that's not failure; that's a holy transition.

Letting go doesn't mean you're faithless. It means you trust that God knows when a chapter has served its purpose better than you do. You can love the memory without living in it. You can honor what it taught you without recreating it. You can bless what's over without blaming yourself for its ending.

There's power in learning to clap for what's over. Because clapping means you recognize completion. You're not applauding the pain; you're celebrating the progress. You're saying, *"That season served me well, but it no longer defines me."*

When you learn to release the familiar, you make room for the *fresh*. When you stop forcing doors to reopen, God starts opening gates you didn't know existed. You stop asking for explanations and start walking in expectation.

I've had to learn that every ending isn't a setback; it's a graduation. It's proof that you've evolved beyond what used to be essential. You can't stay in elementary faith when God is calling you to doctoral destiny. Growth requires goodbye. Some seasons don't end because they failed — they end because they *finished.* And maturity is being able to bow out gracefully, thank God sincerely, and step forward obediently even when your heart still misses what your spirit knows is done.

So today, take a breath and say, "That season served me well." Clap for its end. Celebrate its lesson. And then, with courage and grace, walk into the new thing God has been waiting to begin.

Nothing is lost when it's completed. It simply changes form; from pain into power, from memory into wisdom, from history into heritage.

Captain's Note

There was a time when I didn't know how to let go without feeling guilty. I thought loyalty meant holding on even when peace was long gone. But God kept reminding me: *"Jackie, not every assignment is forever. Some were just to teach you how to build, how to bless, and how to bow out."*

Now I honor the goodbye. I've stopped resurrecting what God buried with purpose because I'd rather live in divine progression than emotional possession. The peace I have today didn't come from everything working out, it came from trusting that what ended had finished its work in me.

Your Reflection Moment

Question 1:
What season in your life might be complete, but you're still calling it broken?

Question 2:
How can you honor what it taught you without reliving what it cost you?

Action Step:
Write a thank-you letter to your last season.
Name what it taught you.
Bless it for what it gave you.
Then close it with:

"I release you with gratitude, not grief." That's the sound of divine completion.

Key Takeaway: *Completion isn't the end — it's evidence that you've evolved. Learn to clap for what's over so you can step freely into what's next.*

"Rejection Is Redirection"

Few things sting the soul like rejection. Especially when you gave it your best: your time, your loyalty, your heart. Rejection has a way of echoing in your spirit long after the moment passes. It makes you question your value, your direction, even your calling.

But here's what I've learned walking with God and leading through life: rejection isn't always a wound; sometimes it's a warning. It's Heaven's way of saying, *"You're too big for this space now."*

For years, I took rejection personally. If people walked away, I blamed myself. If a door closed, I assumed I'd failed. But what I didn't realize was that God wasn't denying me: He was delivering me. He was removing me from spaces that couldn't sustain my next level.

He was closing doors that looked like opportunities but would have become a trap. He was redirecting me from good things that would have kept me from *God things.*

Sometimes rejection hurts because it's pruning pride. We're not just mourning the loss of the opportunity; we're grieving the image of ourselves we built around it. We confuse importance with assignment. And when God removes one, our ego calls it punishment. But His silence isn't neglect; it's navigation.

There were seasons I begged for doors to open that would've buried me under pressure I wasn't prepared to carry. And when those doors stayed shut, I felt forgotten. But looking back now, I realize God was never ignoring me; He was insulating me.

You see, rejection is often protection wearing a disguise. God will withhold access not to deprive you, but to preserve you. He'll say *no* to what's premature so He can say *yes* to what's prepared. He'll remove connections that comfort your flesh but contaminate your faith.

And though it hurts in the moment, His "no" is not a denial, it's direction. It's grace in motion. Every time I've been rejected, I later discovered it was God's way of *rerouting me to alignment.* Because when the wrong people, places, or plans say "no," it frees you to say "yes" to what was always meant for you.

Rejection reroutes. It forces reflection. It refines motives. And if you let it, it will rebuild your confidence in the right foundation, not in validation, but in vision.

"Hear the 'No' Without Losing the Vision"

I used to equate rejection with unworthiness. Now I see it as divine protection dressed in discomfort. When people don't choose you, it's often because God already has. He's reserving your time, your anointing, and your energy for something greater.

When I think about the Titanic, I'm reminded that sometimes being left off the ship is the greatest blessing you'll ever experience. Because not every vessel that looks grand is going where God is taking you, some ships were designed to impress, not to endure.

There's beauty in the 'no' that saves you from the storm you didn't see coming. When God redirects, He doesn't need your permission, just your patience. He's not asking you to understand every closed door. He's asking you to trust the map you can't see.

Faith doesn't mean the route won't change; it means the destination hasn't. You'll know a redirection is divine when peace follows pain. You'll know it's protection when clarity shows up after confusion, and you'll know it's growth when gratitude replaces bitterness. That's when you stop fighting to prove your worth and start resting in God's wisdom.

Captain's Note

As a leader, I've faced rejection in many forms: business deals that fell through, people I mentored who turned away, and opportunities that vanished overnight. Every "no" felt like failure in the moment. But later, I realized each rejection was a setup for realignment.

There were things I prayed for that would have broken me if I had received them. And there were people I thought I needed who would've drained my purpose dry. Now, I thank God for every "no" that didn't make sense at the time but saved my spirit in the long run.

The sting of rejection built my discernment. It taught me to recognize what carries grace and what doesn't. It taught me that my value isn't measured by access, it's measured by assignment.

And when I finally stopped chasing closed doors, I discovered peace waiting at open gates I didn't even have to knock on.

Your Reflection Moment

Question 1:
Where in your life have you mistaken God's protection for rejection?

Question 2:
What opportunities or relationships did you once grieve that now you thank God for closing?

Action Step:
Write down one "no" that still stings.
Next to it, write what it *might* have saved you from.
Pray this: "God, even when I don't understand Your redirection, help me to trust that Your plan is better than my pain."

Then release it. That's not quitting, that's clarity.

Key Takeaway:

Rejection isn't the end of your story; it's the rerouting of it. God's "no" isn't denial, it's divine direction.

"You Can't Heal While Holding On"

Healing requires open hands. But too often, we try to heal while still clinging to what hurt us. We want God to restore us, but we won't release the memory. We pray for peace, yet we keep rehearsing pain. We say we've moved on, but every time something reminds us of the loss, the wound starts bleeding again.

Here's the truth I had to learn: you can't heal from what you won't release. You can't expect fresh oil to pour into a vessel that's still full of resentment. You can't move into your next season dragging the ashes of your last one.

For years, I tried to fix things God was trying to free me from. I tried to rewrite endings He had already signed "finished." Every time I felt broken, I thought the answer was to hold tighter to fix it, prove it, or explain it one more time. But healing doesn't happen through control. It happens through surrender.

Healing begins the moment you stop fighting to understand and start accepting what God already decided. It's not about pretending you're fine, it's about being honest enough to say, *"That hurt me, but it won't hold me."*

Letting go doesn't erase the past; it redeems it. It transforms your pain into wisdom and your wounds into testimony. Because sometimes the very thing you're trying to fix is the thing God is using to free you.

When the Titanic went down, not everyone could carry everything. Some had to throw valuables overboard just to stay afloat. And that's what healing looks like: releasing what's heavy so you can survive what's holy. You can't rise if you're anchored to resentment. You can't hear God clearly while holding on to the noise of disappointment.

You can't walk into purpose while replaying betrayal on repeat. Holding on keeps you in the past; healing invites you into promise. God can't pour new oil into closed fists. He'll wait until you're ready to surrender. Because the miracle doesn't start when you get over it; it starts when you let go of it.

In leadership, we talk a lot about resilience but rarely about release. We celebrate bounce-back stories, not surrender stories. Yet the greatest breakthroughs in my career didn't come from pushing harder; they came from *releasing sooner.*

I had to learn that strength isn't just standing tall; sometimes it's knowing when to sit down and heal. You can't lead effectively when your heart is still hemorrhaging. You can't pour vision from a wounded place and expect it to bear fruit.
And you can't demand clarity from a soul still clouded by pain.

As a leader, I've faced betrayals that cut deep. I've invested in people who later walked away. I've built projects that collapsed after years of work. And in every one of those moments, I tried to fix what was broken until God whispered, *"You're not the healer, I am."*

That truth freed me. It reminded me that healing doesn't mean forgetting, it means forgiving. It means learning to bless what broke you because it introduced you to the strength you didn't know you had.

The Titanic couldn't be saved once it started taking on water. But that didn't mean every life on board was lost. Some things will sink, but you can still be saved if you learn when to let go.

Captain's Note

There was a season in my life when I tried to lead while bleeding. I thought if I just kept working, kept serving, kept helping others, the pain would fade. But all it did was deepen. One day, God stopped me and said, "Jackie, you can't minister from a wound you refuse to acknowledge. You can't be the captain and the casualty." That changed me. Now, I give myself permission to pause. To heal before I rebuild. To breathe before I lead. Because restoration requires stillness.

When I finally let go of the people, expectations, and memories I was gripping, peace rushed in like oxygen after the storm. And I realized: healing isn't the absence of pain, it's the presence of peace.

Your Reflection Moment

Question 1:
What are you still holding on to that God has already healed, but you keep reopening?

Question 2:
Who or what have you been trying to fix instead of releasing to God?

Action Step:
Find a quiet place this week. Write down the things, people, or memories that still trigger pain. Fold the paper and pray over it: "God, I release what no longer serves my peace. I trust You to finish the healing I can't." Then destroy the paper; burn it, shred it, or bury it — as a symbol that the pain no longer owns you. That's how you begin to heal, not by holding tighter, but by letting go completely.

Key Takeaway:

You can't heal while holding on. Let go of what's heavy so you can rise into what's holy. The wound isn't where you end — it's where God begins.

"When God Ends It, Don't Resurrect It"

Some things don't die because the devil attacked them, they die because God ended them.

But because we're emotionally attached, we try to play Savior. We breathe life into what God intentionally let fade. We pour prayer, time, and energy into what no longer carries grace and then wonder why peace never returns.

I've been there. Trying to fix what God already finished. Trying to re-open doors He sealed shut for my protection. Trying to call people back who only left because their part in my story was over. It's painful to accept, but it's freeing once you do: when God ends it, resurrection is not your responsibility.

There's a divine difference between what needs healing and what needs burial. Healing is for what still carries purpose. Burial is for what completed the purpose. If you keep trying to resurrect what God has removed, you'll delay your own recovery. You'll spend emotional energy keeping dead things on life support; old relationships, expired visions, outdated versions of yourself, while your destiny is waiting for you to finally let go.

The hardest truth I've learned is that some endings are acts of mercy, not malice. God doesn't just close doors; He protects destinies. He ends things before they can consume you. He separates you before stagnation sets in. He removes comfort to make room for calling.

But the problem comes when we confuse God's closure with our calling. We think, "If it started in purpose, it must still be my responsibility." Not always. Sometimes purpose evolves. Sometimes God ends the assignment not because you failed but because you finished. And when you try to resurrect it out of guilt or fear, it becomes an idol, something you nurture out of nostalgia instead of obedience.

The Titanic didn't just sink; it stayed sunk. It's still underwater to this day, not because it wasn't great, but because its purpose ended. It served its time, its story, and its warning. Trying to raise it now wouldn't restore it; it would ruin it.

Some seasons are the same way. God doesn't want you to fix the wreckage. He wants you to learn from it and move forward. The beauty of endings is that they create holy space for beginnings. But resurrection attempts keep you chained to history instead of healed in destiny.

When God ends it, don't resurrect it. Don't text it. Don't revisit it. Don't rationalize it. Release it. Let the final period remain a period; don't turn it into a comma. God never writes "The

End" without already preparing "Chapter One" of what's next.

In business, ministry, and life, I've learned that premature resurrection drains divine progress. Every time I tried to hold onto something God was done with, a team member, a plan, a partnership, even a mindset. I found myself carrying weight without wind. Things became harder, heavier, and confusing.

That's how you know grace has lifted, when what once flowed now frustrates you. God doesn't bless rebellion disguised as loyalty. When He's moved on, He expects you to move with Him.

It takes discernment to know when to fight for something and when to faithfully release it. Some relationships deserve repair. Others require release. You have to listen to your peace; it will always tell you the difference.

If peace left, God probably did too. Leaders who grow learn this: holding on can look noble, but obedience looks wiser. You're not abandoning something God ended; you're honoring His boundary. And every time you let go of what's expired, He makes room for what's eternal.

Captain's Note

I once tried to resuscitate an old dream that God had already buried. I prayed harder, worked longer, and begged Him to breathe on it again. But every time I tried, I felt emptier. Until one day, God whispered to my spirit: "Jackie, you're grieving something I already gave closure to. Stop visiting the grave. I'm not there anymore."

That broke me. But it also freed me. Because I realized that the same God who ends things gracefully will also birth new things beautifully. I no longer chase what's left; I trust what's coming.

Your Reflection Moment

Question 1:
What are you still trying to bring back to life that God has already called complete?

Question 2:
How much energy are you spending trying to fix what no longer carries His favor?

Action Step:
This week, identify one area where God has clearly closed a door, a project, a connection, a mindset, or an old dream. Say this prayer aloud: "God, I release what You've finished. I won't resurrect what You've released. I trust You to write the next chapter while I honor the last." Then, stop revisiting what was buried. Stand in your new beginning with open hands and peaceful heart.

Key Takeaway:

When God ends it, don't resurrect it. Resurrection belongs to Him alone. What He finishes in love is never meant to be revived in fear.

"Purpose After Pain"

Pain changes you, but it doesn't have to destroy you. If you allow it, pain can become the *classroom* where God teaches you the most valuable lessons of your life.

When I look back, I realize that every moment of breakthrough in my life was born in a season of breaking. The very experiences that brought me to my knees were the ones that pushed me closer to my calling.

Pain has a way of purifying your motives. It strips away the illusion of control and forces you to depend on grace. It separates the superficial from the sacred. And in that stripping, you discover your *real self*, not the version people applaud, but the one God anointed.

The truth is, you can't walk in full purpose without first walking through pressure. You can't lead with empathy until you've been crushed by something yourself. That's why purpose is often birthed in pain, because pain makes you real, raw, and reliant on God.

When the Titanic went down, not everyone drowned. Some survivors went on to tell their stories, to teach safety, to change maritime law; to make sure what happened to them would never happen to anyone else. Their tragedy became transformation. Their survival became their *service.*

That's what purpose after pain looks like. It's not pretending the ship didn't sink. It's deciding to build lifeboats for others because yours held up.

God doesn't waste wounds. He weaves them into wisdom. He turns the ashes of what broke you into the foundation for what will build you. Your pain is never pointless; it's preparation.

Sometimes the suffering you went through wasn't about punishment; it was about positioning. God was aligning you for something that only the broken version of you could carry. Because cracks let light in and light exposes what was hidden.

When you lead from a healed place, your voice carries power that can't be faked. Your scars become credentials. You stop trying to prove and start trying to *pour.*

Every tear becomes a seed. Every disappointment becomes direction. And every "why, God?" becomes *"thank You, Lord."*

Purpose after pain doesn't mean the pain didn't matter, it means it mattered *enough to change you.* And that change becomes your calling.

I used to believe strength meant never showing pain. But I've learned that transparency *is* strength. People don't connect to perfection they connect to authenticity. And authenticity is born from honesty about where you've been broken.

As a leader, my greatest influence didn't come from my success stories; it came from my survival stories. When I spoke from scars instead of shame, people started to heal through my truth. That's what purpose after pain does, it turns your private struggles into someone else's public strength.

Every business setback, every betrayal, every loss, all of it shaped me into the woman I am today. If I had skipped the pain, I would've skipped the power. If I had avoided the breaking, I would've missed the building.

Now, when I face new pain, I no longer ask, *"Why me?"* I ask, *"What is this trying to teach me?"* Because even in pain, God is still working. He's not punishing. He's preparing.

So don't despise your process. You may not see it yet, but what feels like collapse today will become your testimony tomorrow. And when it does, you'll realize it didn't break you; it *built* you.

Captain's Note

There was a time when my pain silenced me. I didn't want to talk about the losses, the betrayals, the battles. But God reminded me that my silence served no one, not even me. He said, "Jackie, the very thing you're trying to hide is the key to someone else's healing."

That's when I started to see my pain differently, not as proof of failure, but as a tool for ministry. The parts of my story that embarrassed me became the exact stories people needed to hear. Now, I thank God for every broken piece because together, they created a masterpiece.

Your Reflection Moment

Question 1:
What past pain have you tried to erase that might actually be part of your purpose?

Question 2:
How can your scars serve others, not through perfection, but through honesty?

Action Step:
Write down three painful moments that changed you. Next to each one, list how it refined you, what it taught you, revealed, or birthed in you.
Then thank God for the transformation that came through the tears. That's how purpose begins, not after the pain disappears, but when you discover what it delivered.

Key Takeaway:

Pain doesn't disqualify you; it develops you. When you surrender your hurt, Heaven recycles it into purpose.

"The Cost of Ignoring Small Cracks"

The Titanic wasn't destroyed by one big hit it was destroyed by what was ignored. And the same is true in leadership, in business, in relationships, and in faith.

Most ships don't sink overnight. They go down slowly, one overlooked warning, one dismissed concern, one "I'll deal with it later" at a time. Every great collapse begins with a small crack. A crack in communication. A crack in consistency. A crack in integrity. A crack in faith.

But because it doesn't look dangerous in the beginning, we keep sailing. We convince ourselves, *"It's just a little thing."* But little things unaddressed become large things undone. The Titanic didn't have to sink. There were warnings sent. Icebergs reported. But pride said, *"We're unsinkable."* And pride still sinks ships today.

It's not the storm that destroys most leaders; it's the slow leak of unacknowledged issues. It's ignoring burnout until it becomes bitterness. It's overlooking accountability until it becomes a scandal. It's dismissing emotional fatigue until it becomes a spiritual fracture.

God will often send small warnings before major consequences. He'll show you the cracks before they split the hull. But when you're busy proving your strength, you stop checking your structure. You start performing instead of pausing. And performance never protects what pride neglects.

I've learned that every leak has a language. Frustration, fatigue, and resentment they're all signals. The question is: will you listen before it breaks?

As a leader, I've ignored cracks before. Cracks in people. Cracks in planning. Cracks in myself. There were seasons when I felt something wasn't right when my peace was off, but I pressed forward anyway. I told myself, *"It'll work itself out."* But cracks don't heal on their own, they widen.

Leadership requires daily inspection of your foundation. Not because you expect failure, but because you respect longevity. Excellence isn't built by perfection; it's built by maintenance.

You can't pray for a bigger platform if you won't patch your current leaks. You can't ask God for overflow when you haven't repaired what's already draining you. And you can't lead others with authenticity while ignoring the cracks in your own integrity. Ignoring small cracks is expensive. It costs credibility. It costs relationships. It costs peace. And sometimes, it costs destiny.

But here's the beauty of grace: God never exposes what He's unwilling to help you fix.

When He reveals a crack, it's not condemnation, it's construction. He's giving you the chance to reinforce what's still redeemable.

If you humble yourself enough to face the fracture, He'll fortify your faith. If you admit the weakness, He'll rebuild your strength. If you stop pretending the ship is perfect, He'll help you patch what's broken before it sinks.

So, the next time you see a crack in your leadership, in your habits, in your heart, don't ignore it. Inspect it. Address it. Because maintenance now prevents mayhem later. God can handle what's cracked, but He won't bless what's covered up. He heals what's *honest.*

Captain's Note

There was a season when I kept sailing even after God showed me the leak. I was too busy being "strong" to admit I was struggling. Too focused on being the leader everyone leaned on to admit that I needed to lean too.

But leadership without self-awareness is just performance with pressure. And I learned the hard way that if you don't deal with the cracks privately, they will collapse you publicly. Now, I do regular heart checks. Not just for what I lead, but for what I *feel.* I ask God to reveal anything small that could become serious if ignored. Because true maturity isn't just knowing how to build, it's knowing when to repair.

Your Reflection Moment

Question 1:
What "small cracks" in your life or leadership have you been ignoring because they seem manageable?

Question 2:
Where is pride convincing you that "you're fine" when peace keeps saying "you're not"?

Action Step:
This week, do an internal inspection. Ask God to reveal any cracks in your consistency, your integrity, or your boundaries. Write them down. Then pray this: "God, show me what needs mending before it needs saving. Don't wait for the ship to take on water; patch the leak while there's still time.

Key Takeaway: *It's not the iceberg that destroys most visions — it's the cracks we ignore. Humility fixes what pride forgets.*

⚓ Captain's Chapter Reflection: The Power of Letting Go

Releasing What's Heavy to Rise Higher

Every leader eventually reaches the moment where holding on costs more than releasing.

Letting go isn't failure; it's faith. It's the moment you trade control for clarity, and fear for freedom. This reflection is your space to release what's been weighing your leadership, your vision, and your peace.

Reflection Prompts

1. **What am I holding onto that God has already told me to release?**
   Why am I afraid to let it go?
2. **Has my desire to fix something become heavier than my desire to trust God with it?**
3. **What relationships, habits, or responsibilities are draining my peace instead of fueling my purpose?**
4. **How does letting go make room for new opportunities or divine alignment?**
5. **What can I celebrate about what's ending — instead of mourning its loss?**

Captain's Notes

(Use this space to write freely.)

_____

_____

_____

_____

_____

_____

_____

_____

_____

_____

_____

_____

_____

_____

_____

_____

_____

_____

_____

_____

"The higher God wants to take you, the lighter you must travel. Letting go isn't losing — it's making space for what's next."
— *Jacqueline Boatwright-Daus*

CHAPTER FIVE
The Assignment

This chapter is an important turning point.

"Understanding The Assignment"

Before you can lead others effectively, you must first understand *your own assignment.* An assignment isn't just a task; it's a divine directive. It's the specific part you play in God's greater plan, the reason your name was attached to this season.

So many leaders burn out not because they lack strength, but because they've misunderstood scope. They're busy managing everything instead of mastering what they've been called to do. Understanding the assignment means knowing where your authority begins and where it ends. It means saying *yes* to purpose and *no* to distraction.

The Titanic's crew each had assignments; engineers, navigators, stewards, and officers but not everyone *understood* theirs. Some treated the voyage as a job, others as a mission. The difference? Awareness. When the ship hit a crisis, those who understood their role responded with courage and clarity. Those who didn't, panicked.

Leadership requires that same level of self-awareness. You can't protect, build, or grow a vision you don't truly understand. If you don't grasp your why, you'll drown in everyone else's how.

Understanding your assignment begins with intimacy, not with people, but with God. Only He can reveal your purpose and the strategy for fulfilling it. When you understand what you've been called to do, you stop competing and start completing. You stop striving for attention and start walking in anointing. Because clarity is power, and a confused leader creates a confused crew.

When you understand your assignment, you stop chasing validation. You stop comparing your journey to someone else's. You stop saying "yes" to everything that looks good and start committing only to what's *God-ordained.*

Assignment defines boundaries. It tells you what's yours to carry and what's not. Even Jesus didn't heal everyone He encountered; He fulfilled what He was *sent* to do.

Many leaders lose peace because they've taken on weight that doesn't belong to them. They confuse availability with calling. But when you're clear on your assignment, you know that not every opportunity is obligation. Not every invitation is instruction.

Understanding the assignment means knowing the difference between *being busy* and *being built.* It's having the maturity to stay where you're planted until God releases you.

The Titanic reminds us that even the strongest vessel can sink if the mission is mismanaged. The same applies to leadership; when you step outside of your assignment, you expose yourself to unnecessary storms.

Stay focused on what you've been called to do and trust that God will align the right people, provision, and pace to help you finish it.

⏱ Captain's Note

There was a season in my life where I tried to do everything — lead every project, fix every issue, and carry every person. I thought that's what good leadership looked like. But God had to remind me, *"You're not called to do everything, you're called to do what I assigned to you."*

That truth changed me. I realized I was exhausting myself in areas that weren't even my responsibility. I was managing assignments that weren't mine and wondering why I felt drained.

Now, I pray for clarity daily. Before every major decision, I ask, "God, is this my assignment or my distraction?" And when I feel stretched thin, I remind myself: purpose has parameters. My peace is the proof that I'm operating where I belong.

Leadership doesn't require you to do it all; it requires you to do *what you're called to do* with excellence, focus, and faith.

Your Reflection Moment

Question 1:
What responsibilities or roles have you taken on that may not actually be part of your divine assignment?

Question 2:
How do you discern the difference between a good opportunity and a God-given assignment?

Action Step:
Take inventory of your current commitments. Write down what truly aligns with your calling and what simply consumes your time.
Then pray this:

"God, reveal to me the boundaries of my assignment. Give me the strength to release what's not mine and the discipline to complete what is."

This week, practice saying "no" without guilt and "yes" without fear to stay aligned with what you're truly called to do.

Key Takeaway

You can't fulfill a divine purpose with divided focus. Understanding your assignment is what turns your calling into clarity and your effort into excellence.

"Short Vision in A Long Vision Assignment"

You can't build longevity with people who only see the moment. One of the hardest lessons I had to learn as a leader was that I was hiring people based on talent, not *vision.* They could do the work, but they couldn't *see* the work. They were great for a moment but couldn't handle the mission.

When your assignment is long-term and divinely led, you can't afford to fill seats with people who only see as far as Friday. Short vision looks for comfort. Long vision prepares for calling.

I used to think that if I just trained people harder or motivated them more, they'd catch the vision. But you can't teach vision; it's either *caught* or it's *called.* When people have short vision, they work for paychecks. When they have long vision, they work for purpose. Short vision sees tasks; long vision sees transformation. Short vision asks, *"What's in it for me?"* while long vision asks, *"What are we building together?"*

The Titanic wasn't built in a day. It took thousands of hands, years of planning, and incredible innovation. But the tragedy wasn't in the building, it was in the believing. People underestimated risk and overestimated stability. That's what short vision does: it mistakes progress for permanence.

As a leader, it's not enough to have a big dream. You need people who can sustain it. Hiring short-vision people in a long-vision assignment creates a constant cycle of restart. You end up pouring energy into re-explaining, re-training, and re-motivating people who were never supposed to stay.

Short vision can't see beyond convenience. They'll celebrate with you when the ship launches, but they'll question you when the waves rise. They don't leave because they're bad; they leave because they weren't built for endurance.

When your assignment is generational, you have to hire for more than skill; you have to hire for *spirit.* Look for those who:

- Ask about the future, not just the function.
- Take ownership, not offense.
- Speak "we," not "me."

The right people don't need constant convincing; they bring confirmation. When I started aligning my hiring process with my *vision* instead of my *voids,* everything shifted. The wrong people drain energy; the right ones multiply it.

If they can't see where you're going, they'll resent how you lead. That's why discernment is your greatest HR tool.

Captain's Note

I've made the mistake of hiring people who were gifted but not grounded. They looked perfect on paper, sounded confident in the interview, and performed well in the beginning. But when it came time to stretch, they shrank. And the truth is, it wasn't their fault. It was mine. Because I tried to fill a *spiritual position* with a *seasonal mindset.*

I used to pray, *"God, send me help."* Now I pray, *"God, send me alignment."* When I look back, I see the pattern: I was trying to hire people to relieve pressure, not release purpose. But short vision can't carry a legacy; it will always collapse under long-term weight.

Now, I don't just ask what someone *can do.* I ask what they *believe in.* Because I've learned that shared faith and shared vision will outlast skill every time.

Your Reflection Moment

Question 1:
Have you been surrounding yourself with people who see the *mission* or just the *moment?*

Question 2:
What does long vision look like in your organization, and how can you communicate it clearly from day one?

Action Step:
Take inventory of your team. Identify who's adding to the mission and who's just maintaining motion. Then pray: "God, give me discernment to recognize short vision early. Help me build with people who see beyond the now, who see what You're building through me."

Afterward, refine your hiring or leadership criteria. Make "vision alignment" non-negotiable.

Key Takeaway

Short vision builds moments. Long vision builds movements. Choose people who can see beyond their role — who believe in the purpose as deeply as you do.

"The Team and the Assignment"

One of the hardest parts of walking in purpose is realizing that not everyone around you is going to understand it.

Some people love you, but they don't *get* you. They see the moves you're making, the pace you're keeping, the bold decisions you're taking, and to them, it looks extreme. But to you, it's obedience.

When God gives you an assignment, He gives it to *you.* Not to your friends, not to your coworkers, not even to your family. That means there will be seasons where you have to keep building even when no one else believes in what you're building. You'll have to show up with faith while others show up with questions.

The Titanic had an entire crew with assignments; engineers, stewards, officers, musicians but not everyone *understood* the mission. Some were focused on luxury, others on routine, and a few were so confident in the ship's reputation that they ignored the warnings. That's what happens when those around you don't carry the same awareness of what's at stake.

In your own leadership journey, you'll have moments where people question your direction. *"Why are you doing that?" "Why not take it easier?" "Why can't you just stay comfortable?"*

and you'll have to decide whether to slow down for their comfort or stay focused on your calling.

Let me tell you this: when God gives you an assignment, it won't always make sense to people who weren't in the room when He gave it. And that's okay. Because your purpose doesn't require public approval, it requires divine alignment.

There will always be people who can't see what you see, and that's fine; they weren't meant to. God will often hide your full vision from others because He's testing your faith to follow it without validation.

When those around you don't understand the assignment, don't waste your energy trying to explain what was revealed through obedience. Some things aren't meant to be *explained*; they're meant to be *executed.*

Think about it: Jesus walked with people who loved Him, but even they didn't understand the full purpose of His mission until after the cross. That's leadership: moving forward even when those closest to you can't comprehend the weight you're carrying.

You don't need everyone to agree with your calling. You just need to stay in position long enough for God to show them *why* He chose you. Because eventually, the same people who questioned your direction will come back and say,

"Now I see what you meant." But if you pause the mission trying to make them understand it, you'll delay the very thing God anointed you to lead.

Captain's Note

There was a time when I felt frustrated; really frustrated because I was trying to pull people along who just didn't get it. I wanted them to feel the same fire I felt, to move with the same urgency I had. But what God showed me was this:

"You can't make people understand what they're not assigned to carry." That changed everything.

I stopped taking it personally. I stopped explaining every move. And I stopped apologizing for walking in obedience. Some people are connected to your life for companionship, but not for calling. That doesn't make them bad; it just means their capacity is different.

So now, instead of begging people to see the vision, I just build it. I let the results do the explaining. Because obedience always speaks louder than explanation. And when God is steering the ship, you don't need the whole crew to understand the destination, you just need them to keep rowing

Your Reflection Moment

Question 1:
Who in your circle do you keep trying to explain your vision to, even though they're not assigned to understand it?

Question 2:
Are you more focused on being understood by people or being obedient to God?

Action Step:
Take a quiet moment this week to reset.
Pray this prayer out loud: "God, remind me that my assignment doesn't require everyone's approval, just Your direction. Give me peace when I'm misunderstood, and strength to keep building even when others don't believe."

Then commit to one action step that keeps you moving forward, even if no one claps for it yet.

Key Takeaway

Your assignment won't always be understood, but it will always be confirmed. Stay faithful, stay focused, and let your obedience be the evidence.

"Faith To Forge Ahead"

Sometimes, like Abraham, you don't know the end of the vision, but your faith is strong enough to forge ahead.

There will be seasons in your leadership where God gives you a vision without a map. You'll hear the instruction, but not the timeline. You'll feel the call but not see the destination. And it's in those moments that faith stops being a concept and becomes a command.

Sometimes, like Abraham, God says, *"Go,"* without telling you where. And you have to trust that *each step of obedience will reveal the next.*

Abraham didn't need all the details; he needed direction. He walked without knowing the end, because he trusted the One who authored the beginning. That's what real faith looks like. It's not confidence in the path, it's confidence in the promise.

In business, leadership, and calling, there will be days when clarity is limited but conviction is loud. You won't always see how the pieces fit, but you'll feel God urging you to keep building, keep believing, and keep becoming. Faith is forward motion even when you're walking through fog.

Like the Titanic before its voyage, you can have the best plans, the best crew, and the best ship, but if your faith isn't steering, your strength won't sustain you. Faith is what keeps you steady when you can't see the shore.

God doesn't always show you the full picture because He's shaping you through the process. The silence between the steps is where He strengthens your sensitivity.

When you can follow God without knowing the outcome, you've reached a new level of spiritual maturity. Leaders love control. We like blueprints, deadlines, and deliverables. But divine assignments don't always come with clarity; they come with calling.

Faith is what holds you steady when understanding fails. You may not know *how* it's going to work, but you trust *Who* is working.

Abraham didn't have a business plan, a budget, or a board meeting; he had belief. And belief is what built nations. You can have all the strategy in the world, but without faith, you'll fold at the first sign of uncertainty. Leadership through faith means you keep walking even when logic tells you to wait. You keep building even when resources look thin. You keep trusting even when timing doesn't make sense. Because faith doesn't need to see the finish line — it just needs to stay in step with God's pace.

◯ Captain's Note

There have been moments where I felt like Abraham, moving on nothing but a word. God would give me a glimpse, not the guarantee. And I'd say, "Lord, can You at least show me what's next?" And His response was always the same: "If I showed you the end, you'd stop trusting Me for the middle." That's how faith grows.

I've learned that obedience has to come before outcome. When you trust God's character more than your circumstances, you find peace even in the unknown. Every major breakthrough in my life started with a step I didn't fully understand.

Now I tell leaders everywhere, *you don't have to see the whole staircase; just take the step that's in front of you.* Faith doesn't always explain — but it always produces.

Your Reflection Moment

Question 1:
Where has God asked you to "go" without showing you the full plan?

Question 2:
Are you waiting for more details when God's already given you direction?

Action Step:
Write down one area where you've been hesitant because of uncertainty. Then pray this: "God, give me the courage to move forward even without full clarity. Strengthen my faith to trust that if You called me to it, You'll guide me through it."

Take one step this week, even a small one, toward what you've been putting off.

Key Takeaway

Faith isn't knowing how it will end, it's trusting Who began it. Like Abraham, walk even when the map isn't clear, because faith will always lead you where sight cannot.

"Releasing The Lots"

Sometimes the vision can't grow because you're carrying people who were only meant to walk part of the way.

There comes a moment in every leader's journey when you have to make one of the hardest decisions: to release the *Lots* in your life. In Scripture, Abraham loved Lot; they were family, connected by blood and history. But when Abraham obeyed God's command to go to a new land, he took Lot with him, and eventually, their paths had to separate. Lot wasn't evil. He wasn't a villain. He was simply *not assigned* to Abraham's next level.

That's the thing about divine calling: it reveals who's connected to your destiny and who's simply attached to your journey. Everyone who starts with you isn't meant to finish with you. Some relationships are seasonal, not eternal. Some partnerships are divine for a time, but destructive for a lifetime. When you're carrying a heavy vision, even good people can become unnecessary weight. The relationship isn't wrong; it's just *expired.*

Abraham didn't release Lot because of hate; he released him because of *clarity.* Sometimes separation isn't betrayal, it's preservation. You can't walk in full obedience while dragging what God already told you to let go.

If Abraham had kept Lot, his blessing would have been delayed. The same is true for you. You can't take everyone where God is taking you. Vision has a cost, and part of that cost is release.

When the ship is weighted with the wrong people or energy, it loses speed. The Titanic looked invincible, but extra weight and poor discernment led to its destruction. Many leaders today are doing the same: carrying people God told them to bless and *release.*

Releasing the Lots doesn't mean you stop loving them. It means you stop losing yourself trying to carry them. There's a difference between loyalty and lingering. Loyalty supports you; lingering drains you. When God elevates you, He changes your environment, and not everyone is meant to breathe at that altitude. Some people who were comfortable in your last season will suffocate in your next one.

Lot's presence caused confusion in Abraham's assignment. Their people argued, their directions conflicted, and the tension grew, not because of sin, but because of misalignment.

If you're constantly explaining your vision to someone, they're probably not assigned to it. The people who are meant to walk with you don't need convincing; they need direction.

As leaders, we must learn to release with grace. The wrong connection can keep you praying for peace you already had before they arrived. And you'll never see the fullness of God's promise while clinging to those who can't handle your purpose. Sometimes the most spiritual thing you can do is *let go.*

Captain's Note

I've had to release my own Lots. People I loved deeply. People I wanted to see win. But God showed me that love and leadership sometimes move in opposite directions. You can love someone and still recognize they can't go where you're going.

I used to confuse compassion with calling. I thought if I just kept helping, praying, mentoring, or holding on, they'd eventually rise with me. But God whispered, "You're not their savior; you're their seed." Your role was to plant something in their life, not to carry them for the rest of the journey.

That revelation freed me. It hurt, but it healed me, too. Because when I released the Lots, my life got lighter. The vision became clearer. The noise quieted. And I learned this truth: peace always follows obedience. Now, when I feel God shifting relationships, I don't panic — I prepare. Because if He's asking me to release, He's already planning to *replace.*

Your Reflection Moment

Question 1:
Who are the "Lots" in your life, those you love, but who no longer align with your assignment?

Question 2:
Are you holding on out of loyalty, fear, or love, and what is it costing your peace?

Action Step:
Take time this week to ask God, "Show me who is meant for this next chapter and who was meant for the last." Then write down three names or situations that God highlights. Pray a prayer of release, not resentment, and bless them as you let them go.

Releasing isn't rejection; it's redirection.

Key Takeaway

You can't walk into your promise while clinging to people who only understand your past. Releasing the Lots is how you make room for the next level of your purpose.

Captain's Chapter Reflection: The Assignment

Obedience Over Opinion — Staying Faithful to the Call

Every great calling carries weight. The assignment God gives you won't always make sense to others, and that's okay. Your job is not to convince, but to continue. When obedience feels lonely, remember: your faith is building foundations others can't yet see. This reflection invites you to realign your focus and reaffirm your purpose.

Reflection Prompts

1. **Where has God asked me to lead, even when I felt unseen or unsupported?**
2. **Have I been seeking agreement instead of walking in obedience?**
3. **What distractions have pulled my attention away from the true mission?**
4. **How can I serve my current assignment with excellence, even while waiting on elevation?**
5. **Am I protecting the vision or explaining it to people who were never meant to understand it**

Captain's Notes

(Use this space to write freely.)

_____
_____
_____
_____
_____
_____
_____
_____
_____
_____
_____
_____
_____
_____
_____
_____
_____
_____
_____
_____

"Your assignment isn't up for debate — it's up to your obedience. Keep building, even if no one else sees the blueprint."
— *Jacqueline Boatwright-Daus*

CHAPTER SIX

After the Release

This chapter shifts how we move forward

'Leading Lighter'

When God tells you to let go, He's not taking something from you. He's making room for what's next.

There's a silence that follows every release, that strange, still space between *what was* and *what's next.* When you've obeyed God and let go of the people, places, or patterns that were weighing you down, the next test isn't action; it's *stillness.*

After Abraham released Lot, he didn't receive immediate instruction; he received **revelation.** It was only *after Lot separated from him* that God said, *"Now look up."* In other words, *vision expands once the clutter clears.*

Sometimes you can't hear what's next because the noise of what you won't release is still too loud. When you finally let go, God begins to refill the space with strategy, strength, and new sight.

Leadership after release feels different. You lead softer, but stronger. You move slower, but smarter. You're not leading to prove anymore, you're leading to *preserve.*

This is the season where God rebuilds your confidence, restores your focus, and renews your faith. He strips away striving so that peace can lead the way. After release comes renewal, not instantly, but inevitably.

You can't rebuild until you've recovered. Leaders often rush to fill empty spaces, new hires, new projects, and new partnerships, just to avoid feeling the loss. But that's how cycles repeat.

When God allows separation, it's not a punishment; it's preparation. He's resetting your atmosphere for divine alignment.

This season is about reflection, not reaction. Ask yourself: What did that season teach me? What patterns do I refuse to repeat? What boundaries must exist going forward? The ship doesn't rebuild at sea; it docks first. In the same way, your spirit needs stillness before strategy.

Captain's Note

When I had to release people I deeply loved: staff, friends, even family, I thought it would break me. But what I didn't realize was that obedience doesn't break you; it *builds* you.

In that quiet space afterward, I rediscovered my voice. I remembered why I started. And I realized: God doesn't take people away to leave you empty. He does it to clear space for purpose. That's when I started leading differently. I stopped begging people to understand me. I stopped forcing circles to fit into squares. I stopped chasing alignment. I started *attracting* it. Now, when God says "release," I say "thank You." Because I know something greater is coming next.

Your Reflection Moment

Question 1:
What space did releasing someone or something create in your life and how have you filled it?

Question 2:
Are you leading from rest or from reaction?

Action Step:
Take a moment this week to be still. No phone. No meetings. No planning. Just breathe. Pray: "God, thank You for the release. Help me rebuild with wisdom, not worry. Teach me to lead from peace, not pressure."

Then write down three ways you'll protect your peace as you enter this new leadership season.

Key Takeaway

Release is never loss. It's God making space for your next level. When you lead lighter, you lead clearer — and clarity is where vision breathes again.

"Restoring Structure"

God will not bless chaos. Before He adds more, He makes sure what you have can sustain it. After every release, there comes a moment when you must restore structure, when you take everything you've learned in the storm and start putting it back together with strategy and order.

When you've been through a transition, it's easy to confuse movement with progress. But not every step is forward if there's no foundation beneath it. Restoring structure means rebuilding the framework of your leadership, spiritually, mentally, and operationally, so the new vision doesn't collapse under old habits.

God is a God of order. Before He filled the earth, He *formed* it. Before He released the promise, He established the pattern. The same is true in leadership. Before God enlarges your territory, He'll test how well you can steward the space you already have.

When you've released the wrong people, patterns, or priorities, you're left with a clean slate. And here's the truth: what you do next determines how long your peace lasts.

You don't restore by rushing. You restore by *rebuilding right.* That means resetting boundaries, redefining roles, and reestablishing structure, not from exhaustion, but from excellence.

The Titanic failed not because it wasn't strong, but because the structure of vigilance broke down. The systems that could have saved it weren't reinforced. Leadership ignored warnings, and cracks went unchecked. In the same way, we sink when we don't strengthen what's holding us up.

Restoring structure isn't glamorous. It's discipline. It's organization. It's saying, *"I'll fix the foundation before I decorate the deck."* Vision without structure becomes frustration. Faith without framework leads to fatigue.

Restoration requires systems, both spiritual and practical. You can't build a sustainable future on emotional momentum alone. You need alignment between your purpose, your processes, and your people.

Ask yourself:

- Does my calendar reflect my calling?
- Does my team understand their roles?
- Do my systems support peace, or create pressure?

If the answer is "no," then it's time to rebuild.

When God restores structure, He gives you divine blueprints, new methods, better organization, and clearer delegation. He teaches you how to run your vision like a vessel, not a reaction.

True restoration doesn't mean going back to what was; it means building something that can *withstand what's next.*

The ship is only as strong as the structure beneath it. And the leader is only as stable as the systems that sustain them.

Captain's Note

I've learned that restoration is sacred work. It's not loud. It's not flashy. It's often quiet, steady, and behind the scenes.

When I went through seasons of release: people leaving, plans changing, doors closing, I used to rush to rebuild. I thought if I could just start something new, it would erase the sting of what ended. But God had to slow me down and say, "I'm not punishing you; I'm positioning you. Fix the foundation before you dream again." That moment changed my leadership. I stopped building fast and started building faithful. I got organized, clarified my systems, and redefined what excellence looked like.

Now, I don't pray for more; I pray for structure strong enough to hold what's next.

Your Reflection Moment

Question 1:
What systems, habits, or structures in your life or business need to be rebuilt or reinforced?

Question 2:
Have you been praying for increase while neglecting the structure that would sustain it?

Action Step:
Take time this week to examine your foundation. Look at your daily routines, your leadership systems, your boundaries, and your spiritual discipline.

Then pray: "God, show me where my structure needs restoration. Strengthen what's weak, realign what's off, and rebuild me to carry more without collapsing under it."

Then start small; fix one thing at a time. Consistency restores what chaos once broke.

Key Takeaway

Restoration starts with structure. Before God expands your influence, He'll test your integrity. Build it right this time: steady, structured, and Spirit-led.

"Taking Back the Throne"

Every great leader has a throne moment: the place where they must decide whether they'll keep surviving or start reigning again.

There comes a time when life, betrayal, or exhaustion knocks you off your seat of confidence. You once led with boldness, but somewhere between the storms and the shipwrecks, you started shrinking. You started second-guessing your authority, your influence, and your call.

But the truth is, you were never dethroned by circumstance; you simply stepped back to heal. Now, it's time to rise again.

Taking back the throne doesn't mean regaining power; it means reclaiming *position.* It's remembering who you are and what you've been entrusted to lead. It's realizing that your authority was never about control, it was about stewardship. The crown doesn't represent dominance; it represents divine assignment.

Leaders often forget that even in failure, the calling doesn't change. God doesn't revoke leadership; He renews it. The throne is not a symbol of perfection; it's a reminder of perseverance.

Like David, you might've been anointed long before you were accepted. Like Esther, you might've been hidden before you were elevated.

Like Joseph, you might've been rejected before you were recognized. But every detour, every delay, and every disappointment was shaping you for your return to the throne, with greater wisdom and deeper compassion.

The Titanic reminds us that not every fall means finality. Some losses simply reveal the need for new structure, better discernment, and stronger alignment. You don't reclaim the throne by rushing back into motion; you do it by rebuilding the foundation. By leading with humility instead of hurry. By ruling from wholeness, not wounds.

Taking back the throne means you stop apologizing for being called. It means you walk back into your authority, not to prove you're powerful, but to prove God's purpose still lives in you.

You may have been broken, but you were never disqualified. You may have been silenced, but you were never stripped. And now, it's time to sit where you belong: not because of pride, but because of promise.

The crown fits again; this time, perfectly.

Captain's Note

Every leader faces a season when their confidence drifts and their crown feels heavy.
I've been there, questioning my worth, replaying mistakes, and wondering if God could still use me after what broke. But the truth is: God doesn't need perfect vessels; He needs willing ones.

Taking back the throne doesn't mean returning to who you were; it means ruling as who you've become. The storms you survived didn't steal your authority; they strengthened it.
And when you sit again in your rightful place, you don't lead from ego; you lead from empathy. You lead from experience.

So, fix your crown, Captain. The sea still needs your voice.

Reflection

- What caused you to step back from your position — fear, fatigue, or failure?
- Have you mistaken healing for disqualification?
- What does "taking back the throne" look like for you — returning to your calling, your confidence, or your original vision?

Your throne moment isn't about reclaiming control — it's about reclaiming clarity. Sometimes the fall was necessary to teach you how to sit differently, with more grace, more gratitude, and more God.

Takeaway

You were born to lead, not because you're flawless, but because you're faithful. The storms didn't steal your crown; they polished it.

Taking back the throne is not about the spotlight; it's about the assignment. You rise not to prove your strength, but to reflect His sovereignty.

Sit again, not in pride, but in purpose. The kingdom you were meant to lead; your business, your ministry, your vision, is waiting for its captain to take the helm again.

"Fighting the Wrong Battles"

In leadership, every wave looks urgent until you learn which storms are actually assigned to you. Not every crash against your ship is an attack — some are distractions. And not every struggle requires your sword; some simply require your stillness.

The truth is that many leaders aren't losing because they lack vision; they're losing because they're fighting the wrong battles. They've confused movement with progress and reaction with strategy. They're rowing when they should be dipping with buckets; exhausting themselves trying to move forward when the real assignment is to *stay afloat.*

When the Titanic struck the iceberg, chaos broke out. Some crew members tried to fix what couldn't be repaired; others stood still long enough to serve those who could still be saved.

Leadership maturity is knowing the difference between the two. Some seasons call for rowing, pushing, building, and advancing the mission. But others require you to dip water out of the ship just long enough to stabilize what remains. Both are valid forms of leadership, but only wisdom can tell you which one the moment requires.

Fighting battles that aren't yours will always lead to depletion. You'll spend your emotional energy defending what was never meant to be debated. You'll row harder in storms God never called you to sail through. And the harder you row, the more water you take on; not because the sea is too strong, but because your strategy is misplaced.

Understanding the battle means understanding your capacity. It's knowing that sometimes the enemy isn't external, it's internal mismanagement. You can't win every war and still lead in peace. Even the strongest captains must decide when to command and when to conserve.

Some battles are meant to build your faith; others are meant to expose your focus. If you fight everything, you'll lose yourself trying to control outcomes that only obedience can sustain. True leadership means asking, *"Is this wave meant to move me, or to test me?"* Because some waves come to teach you endurance, not engagement.

When you try to fight every battle, you stop leading and start surviving. And survival is not the same as stewardship. God never asked you to save every sailor. He asked you to steer according to His course. The rest is His to calm.

Every great leader must learn the discipline of discernment; knowing which battles to fight, and which to let God handle. Because not every wave is meant to be conquered, and not every storm requires your presence at the helm.

One of the greatest downfalls of leadership is exhaustion from unnecessary warfare. We often pour our strength into defending our position instead of protecting our peace. We engage with distractions dressed as opportunities, and we waste energy trying to convince people who were never assigned to our vision.

The Titanic teaches us something about misplaced focus. While attention was on the ship's luxury and speed, warnings about the ice ahead were dismissed. Leadership failed not just because of what they faced, but because of *what they ignored.* Sometimes the real battle isn't the iceberg; it's arrogance, pride, or the illusion that nothing can touch you.

Understanding your battle means recognizing that not every crisis deserves your full response. Some conflicts are traps designed to pull you off course. Others are tests meant to refine your leadership character. Mature leaders discern the difference. They ask, *"Is this battle building me, or is it draining me?"*

When you fight every fight, you lose the strength for the one that actually matters. Your assignment doesn't require you to fix every problem; it requires you to stay aligned with your purpose. God never called you to fight everything, only to stand firm in what He gave you authority over.

Understanding your battle means protecting your mission from emotional reaction. It's knowing that some storms are meant to pass *without your participation.* And it's trusting that divine justice works better than any argument ever could.

Leaders who last aren't those who fight the hardest; they're those who fight the *wisest.* I had to learn this the hard way: that not every confrontation deserves a captain's time. Some storms exist only to distract you from your course. I used to fight to prove I was right. Now, I fight only to protect what's *righteous.*

Your leadership strength isn't measured by how many battles you enter, but by how many you *avoid* through wisdom. The peace you preserve today becomes the fuel for tomorrow's victory. So before you engage, pause and pray: *"Lord, is this mine to fight or Yours to handle?"*

Because the wisest captains don't waste cannon fire on every ripple in the sea. Discernment is the weapon of mature leaders. When you learn to identify which battles are yours, you stop losing sleep over those that aren't.

Your strength is not in your reaction; it's in your restraint. You were called to lead, not to wrestle with every distraction that calls your name. Understanding the battle means choosing focus over frustration. Because when you stop fighting unnecessary wars, you finally have the energy to win the right ones. Remember: The ocean may be wide, but not every wave deserves your anchor.

Captain's Note

I've learned that leadership isn't about proving strength; it's about preserving peace. There were seasons when I fought every fire, defended every decision, and tried to rescue everyone from their own storms. But I realized I was rowing when I should've been dipping. The goal wasn't to outpace the storm; it was to *outlast it.*

Sometimes you don't need a new plan; you need a new posture. Lay down the oar. Pick up the bucket. Your job isn't always to move forward; sometimes it's to keep the mission from sinking while God stills the waters.

When you understand which battles are truly yours, you lead with clarity, not chaos.
Because wise captains don't fight the sea, they learn to work with its rhythm.

Reflection

- What battles am I fighting that are draining me but not developing me?
- Am I rowing when this season calls for simply dipping and stabilizing?
- Have I mistaken motion for momentum or reaction for revelation?
- Where in my leadership do I need to trade striving for surrender?

Takeaway

The leader who fights everything eventually loses focus on anything. You were not built to battle endlessly; you were built to lead intentionally. When you learn to discern which waves to row through and which to ride over, you'll stop sinking from exhaustion and start sailing in peace.

Remember: even when the ship tilts, the captain doesn't panic; they prioritize. Because great leaders don't just fight the storm… they understand it.

Captain's Chapter Reflection: After the Release

Peace in What's Finished, Strength in What Remains

After the release comes the quiet: that sacred stillness where God confirms what's complete. It's natural to feel uncertain after letting go, but what follows surrender is always strength. This reflection invites you to embrace divine closure, rest from striving, and trust that obedience never returns empty.

Reflection Prompts

1. What did releasing teach me about faith, patience, or timing?
2. Am I at peace with what's finished, or am I still trying to control what God already closed?
3. How has space opened in my life or leadership since I let go?
4. What can I now see clearly that I couldn't while holding on?
5. How can I honor the lesson without clinging to the season?

Captain's Notes

(Use this space to write freely.)

_____
_____
_____
_____
_____
_____
_____
_____
_____
_____
_____
_____
_____
_____
_____
_____
_____
_____
_____
_____
_____
_____

"Every release is a graduation, not a loss. What's surrendered in faith always returns in strength."
— *Jacqueline Boatwright-Daus*

CHAPTER SEVEN

The New Strategy

The entire direction of this journey changes with this chapter.

"Strategy After the Purge"

After God clears the deck, He's not punishing you; He's positioning you. Every great leader faces a purge; that divine shaking where what's unnecessary falls away and what's authentic remains. It's uncomfortable, it's quiet, and it often feels personal. But what you have to understand is this: the purge isn't destruction; it's preparation.

When God purges your environment: people, partnerships, habits, or systems, He's not trying to hurt you. He's trying to make room for *strategy.*

See, strategy is wasted in clutter. You can't hear new instructions while still entertaining old distractions. Before every elevation, there's elimination.

The Titanic's problem wasn't lack of innovation; it was overconfidence and overcrowding. Too many voices, too few visionaries. Too many opinions, not enough obedience. That's what happens when we lead bloated, when we fill our ship with excess instead of excellence.

But after the purge, you gain something priceless: *clarity.* You can finally see what's essential, who's dependable, and where God is directing your next move. Strategy after the purge is sacred work. It's not about rushing to replace; it's about restructuring to *rebuild right.*

After the purge, don't panic, plan.
That's where most leaders fail. They start recruiting out of fear, rebuilding too quickly, or trying to fill every empty space instead of asking, *"God, what belongs here now?"*

When the shaking stops, you don't sprint, you *study.* You examine what cracked, what held, and what has to be done differently this time.

Every purge leaves behind three things: wisdom, warning, and willingness.

- **Wisdom**, the insight that shows you what wasn't working.
- **Warning**, the memory that keeps you from repeating it.
- **Willingness**, the courage to do it better.

That's where strategy is born. It's in that still space after the storm, where you finally have ears to hear and eyes to see. This is when you redefine roles, reestablish values, and refocus the mission. You no longer build out of emotion; you build out of revelation.

If you don't slow down to strategize, you'll repeat the cycle you just survived. God's not just giving you a second chance; He's giving you a smarter one.

Captain's Note

When God purged my circle and stripped away people I thought I needed, I felt empty at first. The rooms were quieter. The phones stopped ringing. The "support" disappeared.

But in that silence, something powerful happened. I started hearing again. I realized that strategy flows best in solitude. God couldn't download next-level instruction because I was too busy managing noise.

When I stopped trying to refill what He emptied, He started to rebuild what I broke. He showed me that *vision without structure is stress,* and *leadership without strategy is survival.*

Now, after every major shift, I don't rush; I *review.* I look at what's left, what remains, and what's ready to grow. And I ask: "God, what's the strategy for this season? Who belongs on this ship now?" Because every new level requires a new structure, and strategy is what keeps your ship from sinking twice.

Your Reflection Moment

Question 1:
What did the last purge reveal about your patterns or people?

Question 2:
Have you started rebuilding too soon, or are you allowing God to give you fresh strategy first?

Action Step:
Before you plan your next move, take a day to *audit your structure.* Look at your systems, staff, and spirit. Ask yourself honestly: *What's still aligned, and what's still attached?*

Then pray: "God, give me a divine strategy for this next season. Teach me to rebuild with precision, not panic. Let wisdom lead every decision I make from here on."

Then write out your top three priorities for the next quarter, not from a place of pressure, but from purpose.

Key Takeaway

After the purge, don't rush to fill the emptiness; use it to design your next era. Strategy is the reward of obedience.

"Restoring the Vision"

Vision is the soul of leadership. It's what gives direction when the sea looks endless and courage when the storm refuses to pass. But what happens when the vision you once saw clearly becomes blurred by disappointment, fatigue, or betrayal?

There comes a point in every leader's journey when the waters of adversity cloud your sight. You remember what God showed you, but not how it felt to believe it. The dream is still there, but the fire has dimmed. The ship hasn't sunk, but your confidence has taken on water.

Restoring the vision isn't about creating something new; it's about *seeing again* what was always there. It's reclaiming the focus you lost while fighting battles you never asked for. It's understanding that storms don't destroy divine purpose; they strengthen your spiritual sight.

Sometimes, the delay wasn't denial; it was development. God had to let the wind blow to show you who was truly anchored beside you. He had to let the fog roll in so you'd stop relying on visibility and start relying on His voice.

Vision fades when you stop looking up. The moment your eyes shift from divine instruction to human interference, you start steering by sight instead of faith. And nothing derails vision faster than exhaustion paired with doubt.

But here's the truth: even when your focus falters, the vision doesn't die. What God births in faith cannot drown in failure. It may go quiet, it may rest, it may even be hidden, but it will not disappear.

Like the Titanic, your mission may encounter collision, but collision doesn't mean conclusion. The same hands that built the ship can restore it. The same God who gave you the blueprint can breathe new life into it.

Restoring the vision begins with remembering the "why." Before there were results, before there were people, before there was applause; there was purpose. Go back to that place. Revisit your original encounter with the vision. Remind yourself of what God said, even if no one else remembers. Because when you restore vision, you restore leadership. And when you restore leadership, you restore destiny.

Captain's Note

Leaders lose sight not because they stop believing, but because they stop beholding. You can't steer what you can't see, and you can't see what you've stopped seeking. In seasons when the vision feels blurred, I've learned to return to the Source. The moment I stop trying to fix the outcome and start listening again to the original instruction, clarity returns.

Don't be afraid to revisit the wreckage. Sometimes, God hides pieces of the new vision in the ruins of the old. The vision hasn't failed; it's being *refined.*

Reflection

- Has your vision become buried under busyness, burnout, or disappointment?
- What were the first words God spoke to you about this mission, and do they still guide your steps today?
- Are you leading from clarity or from confusion?

Restoring the vision means restoring your spiritual sight; shifting from what was lost to what's still possible. It's looking through the fog and remembering the promise that got you here.

Takeaway

The enemy can't steal your purpose; he can only blur your perception of it. Restoration doesn't begin with movement; it begins with *focus.* Look again. Listen again. Believe again. The vision isn't gone, it's waiting for you to see it clearly once more

"Rising After the Storm"

Every leader faces a storm. It's not a question of *if*, it's a question of *when.*
The storm doesn't always announce itself; sometimes it arrives silently, disguised as betrayal, loss, exhaustion, or change. But no matter how it comes, every storm carries a purpose: to strip away what's shallow so what's sacred can stand.

The aftermath of a storm is where leadership maturity begins. When the winds calm and the noise fades, you stand surrounded by what survived. And in that moment, you realize, the storm didn't come to destroy you. It came to *reveal you.*

Rising after the storm is not about pretending it didn't hurt. It's about acknowledging the pain, then choosing not to stay in it. You rise, not because you're unbroken, but because you're *unbeaten.* You've been shaken but not shattered. Drenched, but not drowned. Pressed, but not destroyed.

The Titanic may have gone down, but its story still rises. The wreckage remains not as a symbol of failure, but as a reminder of the cost of ignoring warning signs and underestimating divine alignment. Your own storms teach the same; they refine your faith, sharpen your discernment, and remind you who truly commands the waves.

When God allows a storm, He also appoints a season of rising. The winds that tried to break you become the same winds that lift you higher. The tears that once clouded your eyes start watering the seeds of a new vision. You realize that what fell apart wasn't punishment, it was preparation.

Rising after the storm means letting go of bitterness and picking up belief again. It's standing on the deck of what's left and saying, *"This isn't over."* Because storms may silence for a night, but resurrection always speaks in the morning.

The leader who rises after the storm carries a different kind of strength: quiet, steady, and spiritual. You don't need to prove who you are anymore; you've weathered enough waves to know. Now, your peace speaks louder than your pain, and your wisdom leads stronger than your words. You are no longer surviving; you are *sailing again.*

Captain's Note

When I look back over the storms I've survived, the criticism, the losses, the tears, I realize they didn't take me under. They taught me how to breathe differently. They taught me how to pray in the wind and listen in the thunder.

Storms don't make weak leaders; they reveal strong ones. And when the sea finally calms, you'll notice something: you didn't just survive, you *shifted.* You became more anchored, more discerning, more determined. The winds that once terrified you now testify for you. You don't rise because you're fearless, you rise because you're faithful.

Reflection

- What did the storm take from you, and what did it *teach* you in return?
- Have you allowed the pain to make you bitter, or have you let it build your belief?
- What does rising look like for you in this season, rebuilding, releasing, or resting?

Every storm resets priorities. It removes what's unnecessary and reveals what's eternal. You rise by remembering who you are and whose you are.

Takeaway

The storm was never sent to drown you; it was sent to develop *you. Every wind had a reason, every wave had a lesson, and every silence had a purpose. Rising after the storm is the mark of a mature leader — one who's learned that faith is the true lifeboat and obedience is the only compass that never fails.*

You've been tested, but now you're trusted. You've been shaken, but now you're strengthened. You've been through the storm; now it's time to sail again.

"Moving Forward with Clarity"

Clarity isn't found in motion; it's found in meaning. There's a moment after every storm when the water finally calms, but it's not peace if you're still confused about where to go next. Moving forward doesn't start with speed. It starts with clarity.

Clarity is leadership's compass. It keeps you from drifting back into old patterns disguised as new opportunities. It's what separates reaction from revelation, and busyness from purpose.

When the Titanic set sail, it had momentum but not mindfulness. The ship was powerful, fast, and admired, but it wasn't cautious. That's what happens when motion outruns meaning.

As leaders, we often mistake exhaustion for progress. We move so fast trying to "fix" what fell apart that we forget to *focus* on what's next. But clarity isn't about doing more, it's about seeing better. After the purge, after the rebuild, after the lessons, clarity becomes your greatest leadership asset.

You finally stop asking, *"What do I need to do?"* and start asking, *"What am I called to accomplish?"*

Clarity is not the absence of chaos, it's the ability to see purpose in it. When you move forward with clarity, you don't waste energy on people or projects that no longer align. You stop overexplaining yourself to those who don't have your assignment. You stop trying to prove and start learning to *preserve.*

Clarity demands discipline. It requires you to be honest about what's working, what's not, and what needs to change, even if that means leaving comfort behind.

To move forward with clarity, you must:

- **Revisit your why.** Remind yourself what God originally told you to do before opinions got loud.
- **Refine your focus.** Everything can't be a priority; peace is found in precision.
- **Rebuild your rhythm.** Set new habits that support your next season, not your old one.

When your vision becomes clear, your pace becomes intentional. You stop chasing what's urgent and start protecting what's important.

Clarity transforms pressure into purpose. It gives you permission to stop surviving and start *strategically thriving.*

Captain's Note

There was a season in my life where I was moving constantly; meetings, projects, ideas, but I felt spiritually stuck.
It looked like progress on paper, but in my spirit, it felt like noise.

Then one day, God said something that stopped me in my tracks: "You're busy, but you're not building. You're moving but not multiplying." That's when I realized, clarity is currency.
Without it, you spend energy with no return.

So, I slowed down. I stopped chasing momentum and started chasing meaning. I asked God to show me what mattered *now.* He didn't give me a new plan, He gave me a new *perspective.*

I saw who was supposed to stay, what needed to stop, and how to move forward without losing myself. And that's the power of clarity, it doesn't just tell you *where* to go, it reminds you *who you are* as you go.

Your Reflection Moment

Question 1:
What areas of your leadership feel active but not effective?

Question 2:
Where have you been confusing movement with momentum or momentum with meaning?

Action Step:
This week, take one quiet hour to reflect on where you're headed.
Ask God: "What's my next *right* move, not my next *fast* one?"

Write down three things that no longer align with your clarity. Then, replace them with three intentional actions that serve your mission today.

Don't move because it's time, move because it's *clear*.

Key Takeaway

Clarity is the leader's true compass. Once you see clearly, you'll stop chasing waves and start charting waters.

"Why the Struggle Was Necessary"

Nobody prays for struggle. We don't wake up asking God for stretching seasons, for loss, for pruning, for disappointment, or for long nights where the only thing we have left to hold is faith.

But I learned something I didn't want to learn and maybe you did, too: ease doesn't develop leaders, pressure does. The moments that hurt the most ended up shaping the parts of me I needed the most. The seasons I thought were destroying me were actually disciplines disguised as discomfort.

Struggle introduced me to the strength I didn't know I had. It revealed faith I didn't know I was still holding onto. It exposed fears I had been carrying and excuses I had been hiding behind. Pain didn't disqualify me from purpose; it prepared me for it.

If everything had come easily, I would've taken the blessing for granted. If every door had opened on command, I would've believed it was my hand, not His grace. If every person had stayed loyal, I would've trusted comfort more than calling.

The struggle stripped the noise... the attachments... the illusions... the pride that whispered, "You can do this part without God."

And just like that, I learned that pressure wasn't punishment, it was preparation. Preparation for deeper discernment. Preparation for leadership with backbone and sensitivity. Preparation for decisions that require spiritual maturity and not emotional reaction.

People see the story now, the confidence, the clarity, the calling, but they didn't see what it cost. You don't get oil without pressing. You don't get elevation without endurance. You don't get anointing without adversity that proved you could carry it.

The struggle was necessary because the version of you that could "survive" success wasn't born yet. You had to be tested, not to see if you would break, but to prove what God built inside you won't.

Some people drown in shallow water because they never learned to breathe under pressure. You learned. And because of that? You're not just operating in purpose; you are anchored enough to hold it.

This season didn't prepare you for *public victory*; it prepared you for private stability. So, when elevation arrives, your integrity rises with it, not your ego. You are not strong because you avoided struggle. You are strong because you survived what others would have surrendered to. That's why the struggle was necessary. It wasn't breaking you. It was building your capacity. *The Breaking Was Building Something in You.*

Captain's Note

I didn't understand the breaking when I was in it. I only understood once I walked out of it differently. I didn't just come out wiser; I came out lighter. I didn't just come out stronger; I came out surrendered. And surrender is where real strength begins.

If you are in a stretching season right now, breathe. God isn't trying to take something from you, He's preparing to trust you with something bigger.

You don't have to like the pressure to be shaped by it. Just stay teachable. Stay humble. Stay anchored. Every struggle has purpose, and you're going to thank God for this one soon.

Reflection Questions

1. What part of my character or faith was strengthened through the struggle?
2. What did the difficult season teach me about myself that the easy season never could?
3. Which attachments or beliefs did God remove so I could grow?
4. How did this struggle deepen my prayer life, patience, or discernment?

Takeaway

You were not weakened; you were forged. Everything God is building in you required this version of you, the one who endured, evolved, and emerged. Your struggle was not a setback. It was proof that God trusted you with growth others never reach.

And now? You don't just carry vision: You carry capacity.

Captain's Chapter Reflection: The New Strategy

Hearing Fresh Instructions After the Storm

When God shifts your strategy, it isn't rejection, it's redirection. The vision doesn't change, but the method might. True leaders understand that storms don't end the mission; they simply require a new map. This reflection invites you to listen again, plan with faith, and move forward with courage.

Reflection Prompts

1. What strategies once worked that no longer align with where God is leading me now?
2. Am I flexible enough to change course when the Spirit shifts direction?
3. How can I make space for new ideas, voices, and divine creativity?
4. What lesson from the last season is meant to shape the next?
5. Have I prayed for clarity and then trusted the answer enough to act on it?

Captain's Notes

(Use this space to write freely.)

_____

_____

_____

_____

_____

_____

_____

_____

_____

_____

_____

_____

_____

_____

_____

_____

_____

_____

_____

_____

_____

_____

"When God changes the strategy, it's not a setback
— it's an upgrade in direction. Don't fear the new
map; it's guiding you toward greater territory."
— *Jacqueline Boatwright-Daus*

CHAPTER EIGHT
THE REBUILT BLUEPRINT

In this chapter, it all comes together!

"Leading After the Wreckage"

There's a kind of leadership no one prepares you for: the kind that begins after everything falls apart. When the ship tilts, everyone looks to the captain. But when the ship breaks, everyone looks for the exit. And there you are, standing in the wreckage; not just leading, but *learning* what leadership truly means when nothing is left but pieces.

Leading after the wreckage isn't about picking up where you left off. It's about finding purpose in what survived. It's about understanding that the loss doesn't disqualify you; it *redefines* you. There's a sacred stillness that follows every storm. The sound of silence after chaos teaches what applause never could. In that quiet, you realize that leadership isn't proven by how loud you shouted commands in crisis, but by how faithfully you rebuild once the waters calm.

The Titanic didn't fail because the ship wasn't strong; it failed because too many people trusted reputation over readiness. That's the warning for leaders: success can make you comfortable, and comfort can make you blind. Sometimes, wreckage is mercy in disguise: God breaking apart what was built without His full direction.

Leading after the wreckage means choosing to *see differently.* You stop asking, "Why did this happen?" and start asking, "What am I supposed to learn?" You realize that God doesn't abandon leaders in the wreckage: He meets them there. He rebuilds through those who still believe, even with trembling hands and tear-streaked faces.

Every great leader faces a shipwreck moment: Moses in the desert, Paul after the storm, Peter after the denial. Each found purpose not in perfection, but in persistence. What looked like an ending was simply a restructuring. So, when the vision breaks, don't quit, *recalculate.* When the followers scatter, don't despair, *refocus.* When the dream collapses, don't curse it, *consult Heaven again.*

The wreckage isn't proof that you failed. It's evidence that God is redirecting the vessel. What you rebuild after the breakage will be stronger, purer, and wiser because this time, it will be anchored in revelation, not reputation.

Captain's Note

Every wreck carries a revelation. If you lead long enough, you'll face the kind of breaking that no manual can teach you through. The question isn't whether you'll encounter wreckage; it's whether you'll rise from it.

In my own leadership journey, I've learned that the wreck doesn't end the mission; it humbles it. It strips away pride, noise, and illusion until all

that's left is truth.
And truth, though painful, is what sets leaders free.

You'll know you've matured in leadership when you can thank God not only for what you built, but for what He allowed to break. Because some ships were never meant to finish the journey, they were meant to teach you how to swim.

Reflection

- What lessons are hiding in your wreckage that success never taught you?
- Are you leading from restoration or from resentment?
- How has failure shaped your faith, focus, and the way you now lead others?

Sometimes God allows the breaking to rebuild you without the baggage. What you salvage from the wreckage becomes sacred material — the wood and steel of your next assignment.

Takeaway

Leading after the wreckage requires courage to believe that what's left is enough. You may not have everything you started with — but you have everything you need to begin again.
The most powerful captains aren't the ones who never crashed; they're the ones who learned to steer again with wisdom born of the waves.

"The Leader's Compass"

Every great ship has one tool that determines its destiny: the compass. It doesn't shout, it doesn't argue, and it doesn't change its direction because of the storm. It simply points *true north*.

As leaders, we all need a compass. Not the kind that measures profit or popularity, but the kind that measures *purpose*. A compass guided by conviction, not convenience. Because in leadership, it's easy to drift. A few degrees off in focus can take you miles away from where God intended you to go.

Your compass is your inner guidance; the combination of faith, integrity, and discernment that keeps you aligned with your calling when emotions, criticism, or exhaustion tempt you to veer off course. It's not about what feels right; it's about what *is* right in God's eyes.

Every storm tests your compass. The waves of distraction will rise, the winds of doubt will howl, and the noise of the crowd will demand that you turn the ship. But if you steer by emotion, you'll shipwreck the mission. A true leader must be grounded enough to hear God's whisper over the world's roar.

There were officers aboard the Titanic who saw warning signs, but their compass, their sense of urgency and caution, had been dulled by overconfidence. They thought reputation would keep the ship afloat. But success without sensitivity to danger is how great vessels sink.

Your compass doesn't just keep you moving; it keeps you *centered*. It reminds you that speed means nothing without direction. And while storms may push you, the compass ensures you always find your way back to purpose.

When God gives you a vision, He also gives you the internal compass to protect it. It's that quiet conviction that says, "Don't go that way," even when everyone else does. It's the still small voice that reminds you to pause, pray, and wait before reacting.

Without that compass, leaders make emotional decisions that create long-term damage. But with it, you lead from alignment, not anxiety. You move from reaction to revelation, steering not by impulse, but by insight.

Captain's Note

Every leader needs a moment to recalibrate. You can't navigate by feelings; they shift like tides. You can't steer by applause; it fades like echoes. You must lead by direction, by your divine compass.

In my journey, I've learned that the compass of leadership isn't found on your desk; it's found in your spirit. It's your ability to say, "I will not drift," even when it feels easier to follow the current. When your compass points to faith, you'll never lose your way, even if you lose your map.

Reflection

- What's guiding your decisions right now, pressure or purpose?
- When was the last time you stopped to recalibrate your compass before moving forward?
- Are your daily actions aligned with your divine north, or are you drifting toward convenience?

Your compass is only as accurate as your last alignment. You must stop often enough to make sure your direction still matches your destiny.

☺ Takeaway

True leadership isn't about speed, it's about direction. The storm can shake your sails, but it cannot shift your compass when it's set by faith.

When you lead with conviction, you'll never be lost for long. And when you follow God's coordinates, even your detours become divine redirection.

"Blueprints And Boundaries"

Strategy sets the direction, but boundaries protect the destination. Once God gives you strategy, the next step is to build, not emotionally, but *intentionally*. Blueprints and boundaries are what turn inspiration into infrastructure. Without them, even the strongest vision will crumble under pressure.

Think of a blueprint: it's precise, detailed, and orderly. It shows what goes where, what connects to what, and what can't be moved. That's how your leadership must operate after the purge: clearly, carefully, and under divine instruction.

A *blueprint* tells you what to build. A *boundary* tells you what to protect. Together, they sustain everything you're called to create.

Most leaders fail not from lack of vision, but from lack of boundaries. They pour wisdom into chaos, energy into dysfunction, and end up drained because they never drew the lines that keep purpose safe.

The Titanic was built from a powerful blueprint, but ignored boundaries. Corners were cut. Warnings were dismissed. Pressure was underestimated. What started as brilliance ended in breakdown. That's what happens when you have plans without protection.

Every divine assignment requires a structure that honors both God's order and your own well-being. Vision grows best when guarded.

After the purge, you can't build the same way you used to. The old model can't hold the new mandate. This is your *architect season*, where every detail matters and every decision carries weight. Your blueprint determines what you build. Your boundaries determine what lasts.

Ask yourself:

- Do I have clear systems in place that reflect where I'm going?
- Are my daily routines aligned with my long-term vision?
- What drains me that I keep allowing access to?

Boundaries are not walls; they're filters. They keep what's sacred from being scattered. When you don't have them, you end up protecting everyone else's peace while neglecting your own.

Leadership doesn't mean being available to everything; it means being accountable to your assignment. Blueprints are obedience in action. Boundaries are wisdom in practice. One builds the dream; the other keeps it from collapsing.

If you want to lead at the next level, you must learn to say *no* strategically, not emotionally.

Because everything that demands your attention doesn't deserve your attention.

Captain's Note

When I started rebuilding after a major shift, I realized my issue wasn't vision, it was *volume.* Too many people, too many projects, too much noise. I was busy but not balanced. I was leading effectively but living exhausted.

God had to show me that *success without structure is just chaos in disguise.* So, I paused. I reorganized. I restructured. I wrote down what mattered most, and then I built boundaries around it. I stopped saying "yes" out of guilt and started saying "no" out of growth. And you know what happened? Peace returned. Productivity increased. Purpose expanded.

Now, I treat my boundaries like I treat my business; they get managed, maintained, and respected. Because you can't lead freely if you're living frantically.

Your Reflection Moment

Question 1:
Where do you need to rebuild structure, not in your schedule, but in your spirit?

Question 2:
What boundaries have you been afraid to set because you're worried about how others will react?

Action Step:
Take time this week to draw your new blueprint; literally. Sketch or write down your next-level structure: your top priorities, protected times, key roles, and personal non-negotiables.

Then pray: "God, give me the wisdom to build what You've designed, and the discipline to guard what You've entrusted."

As you do, remember structure doesn't restrict, it secures.

Key Takeaway

Blueprints create vision. Boundaries preserve it. Build with clarity and protect with courage — because what you're constructing now is meant to last.

"Faith Over Feelings"

Feelings are powerful, but they are not permanent. They shift like tides, rise like waves, and can drown your clarity if you let them steer your ship.

Faith, on the other hand, is steady. It doesn't need to see the shore to believe it's there. And that's what mature leadership requires, *a decision to lead by faith, not by feelings.*

When I first started leading, I thought maturity meant keeping my emotions hidden. But true maturity isn't suppression, it's stewardship. It's learning how to honor your emotions without handing them the wheel.

Every great leader must learn the difference between reaction and response. Reactions are emotional. Responses are intentional. Reactions come from fear. Responses come from faith.

When emotions lead, chaos follows. When faith leads, clarity returns. There were seasons in my life where I made decisions from hurt, not healing. From fear, not faith. And I learned quickly: feelings make poor captains.

The Titanic was built to withstand waves, but not arrogance. Likewise, we're built to handle pressure, but not pride. And emotional immaturity often hides behind pride. It says, *"I'll do it my way."* But faith says, *"God, I trust Your way, even when I don't understand it."*

Faith over feelings isn't about pretending you're unshaken, it's about remembering Who steadies you. You can cry and still continue. You can doubt and still do. You can feel afraid and still lead faithfully. That's maturity; moving forward even when your emotions beg you to stop.

Emotional maturity in leadership is learning to pause before you respond. To pray before you speak. To reflect before you react. Maturity doesn't silence emotion — it filters it through wisdom. It knows when to act from the heart and when to wait for peace.

When people disappoint you, maturity doesn't let offense run the meeting. When stress rises, maturity doesn't let panic dictate the plan. When betrayal stings, maturity doesn't let bitterness build a home. Faith says, *"This hurt, but it didn't end me."* It reminds you that pain is a moment, not your identity.

As leaders, we must be the calm in the storm, not the storm in the calm. And that requires emotional discipline; the ability to stand still in spirit while everything around you shifts.

There will be times when you feel unseen, unappreciated, or misunderstood. That's when maturity whispers, *"This isn't about validation; it's about assignment."*

You can't walk in faith and feed every feeling at the same time. Eventually, one will lead and the other will follow. Choose faith. Because faith sees beyond the now, it sees the next.

The Titanic failed not because the ocean was too strong, but because leadership ignored warning signs. Likewise, when we let emotion override discernment, we steer straight into avoidable wrecks. Maturity knows how to listen to God's caution, even when feelings crave motion.

Captain's Note

There were seasons I let my feelings lead, and every time, I ended up exhausted. Hurt made me reactive. Disappointment made me defensive. Pressure made me impatient. But maturity came the day I realized: "My emotions are valid, but they're not my vision."

Faith keeps me focused when feelings fluctuate. It anchors me when fear rises. It reminds me that obedience is greater than opinion, even my own. Now, before I make decisions, I ask:

- Am I responding from emotion or instruction?
- Am I moving from fear or faith?

That small pause has saved me from big mistakes. Because leadership through maturity isn't about never feeling it's about never letting feelings become your final authority.

Your Reflection Moment

Question 1:
Where have you been reacting from emotion instead of responding through faith?

Question 2:
What situation in your leadership journey requires maturity over movement right now?

Action Step:
The next time you feel triggered or pressured to act quickly, pause. Breathe. Pray this: "God, help me to feel it but not be led by it. Teach me to respond through faith, not frustration. Let maturity be my anchor and peace be my pace." Then make your move, not from emotion, but from conviction.

Key Takeaway:

Faith doesn't deny feelings; it disciplines them. Mature leadership listens to emotion but follows conviction.

"Growing Through What Tried to Break You"

Growth rarely happens on the mountaintop. It happens in the dark, in the breaking, in the questioning, in the in-between where nothing makes sense but faith.

Every strong leader I've ever met carries a scar. Not from failure, but from *formation:* Because leadership is forged in fire, not applause.

The things that tried to break you were never meant to bury you. They were meant to build you differently. When I look back over my life and my businesses, the seasons of betrayal, burnout, financial strain, even isolation, I can see now what I couldn't then: God wasn't breaking me down; He was *breaking me open.*

He was pruning pride, stretching capacity, and removing what couldn't go where I was going. Every "no" refined me. Every setback revealed something sacred. Every tear baptized me for the next level of leadership.

You don't become the leader who changes lives by avoiding pain; you become that leader by surviving it with grace. Just like the Titanic, there were times my vision felt unstoppable, until I hit something that tested my structure. But unlike the Titanic, I refused to sink. Because pain isn't always punishment, sometimes it's preparation. Growth begins the moment you stop asking, *"Why me?"* and start asking, *"What is this teaching me?"*

If you can turn your pain into purpose, your weakness into wisdom, and your failures into faith, you'll lead with an authority that can't be imitated: Because you'll be leading not from theory, but from testimony.

Every great leader faces a breaking point. It's the moment when you realize your title can't fix your tears and your success can't silence your soul. It's when you learn that true leadership isn't about perfection, it's about perseverance.

The moment you stop running from what hurt you and start learning from it, the pain loses its power. You begin to grow differently. You lead with compassion instead of comparison. You build with discernment instead of desperation. And suddenly, what tried to destroy you becomes what defines you.

There were days I didn't think I'd make it. Days where I led through heartbreak, smiled through stress, and showed up when I wanted to stay hidden. But even then, God was teaching me that strength isn't the absence of breaking, it's the decision to rebuild wiser.

Growth through adversity requires two things:

1. **Perspective** — seeing pain as instruction, not interruption.
2. **Patience** — allowing the lesson to mature before you move.

Leaders who grow through pain don't just bounce back; they build better. They stop blaming the storm and start mastering the wind. Because what once hurt you now helps you lead.

Captain's Note

I used to think being broken meant I was failing. Now I know being broken meant I was *becoming.* Every time life cracked me open, more wisdom came out. Every time I was overlooked, God was overseeing something greater. And every time I was pushed down, I learned how to plant deeper.

You can't become a transformational leader without transformational pain. That's the cost of calling and the reward of resilience. So, when you find yourself in a season that feels like it's falling apart, don't panic, you're not breaking down, you're *breaking through.*

Your Reflection Moment

Question 1:
What situation tried to break you, but instead became your greatest teacher?

Question 2:
How can you use that experience to lead others with empathy and authority?

Action Step:
Write down one of your hardest seasons.
Underneath it, list three things it taught you about yourself, leadership, and God.
Read it aloud and thank Him; not for the pain, but for the *product* that came from it.

Then remind yourself: growth doesn't always feel good, but it's always good *for* you.

Key Takeaway:

True leadership isn't avoiding what breaks you; it's learning how to grow through it, so others see God's strength where your weakness once lived.

"Sometimes You Can't Recover, But You Can Always Rebuild"

There are some storms you don't walk away from the same. Some losses you don't "get over." Some endings that change you so deeply that recovery isn't possible; only *rebuilding* is.

For years, I prayed to recover what I lost. Relationships. Opportunities. Moments that slipped through my fingers. But recovery implies returning to what was. And the truth is, sometimes God doesn't want you to go back. He wants you to *build forward.*

The Titanic was never recovered. Pieces were found. Memories preserved. Lessons learned. But the ship itself it stayed where it fell. And yet, its story still built something: awareness, reform, reverence. Its fall birthed change. Its loss, built legacy.

That's what rebuilding looks like. It's choosing to turn ruin into revelation. It's accepting that while you may never have the "before" again, you can still create something purposeful *after.*

When you lose something that mattered: a dream, a person, a version of yourself, your instinct is to want it back. But sometimes God removes not to replace, but to *repurpose.* He uses what's broken to birth what's better. Recovery focuses on restoration. Rebuilding focuses on transformation. And transformation is where real leadership begins.

Every strong leader carries a story of rebuilding. You don't become wise by winning; you become wise by *withstanding*. There will be seasons that take your breath, your confidence, even your certainty. But those seasons are where your foundation gets redefined.

When the plan fails, rebuild the purpose. When the dream ends, rebuild the direction. When the team leaves, rebuild the vision, even if you have to build it alone.

I've had to rebuild more times than I can count. Rebuild businesses. Rebuild faith. Rebuild myself. But every time, I found that rebuilding doesn't start with my hands, it starts with my heart.

Rebuilding requires courage, the kind that doesn't wait for conditions to be perfect.
You don't wait for the storm to stop; you start gathering wood in the rain. You start again, even if your hands are trembling.

God doesn't promise recovery; He promises renewal. He said, *"Behold, I make all things new,"* not "I make all things the same." So, if what you lost doesn't come back, it's not rejection, it's redirection. You're being asked to build what couldn't exist before the breaking. Rebuilding is the ultimate act of faith. It says, *"I still believe in tomorrow, even after today collapsed."*

Captain's Note

When I look back on everything that's fallen apart in my life: partnerships, plans, seasons, even people, I see now that none of it was wasted. Each loss cleared space for something that aligned better with who I was becoming.

I wanted to recover my comfort; God wanted to rebuild my character. I wanted to regain the familiar; He wanted to reveal the future.

At first, it hurt. I missed the way things were. But recovery would've only returned me to a version of myself that couldn't handle where He was taking me.

Now, I don't pray to recover. I pray to rebuild: stronger, wiser, softer, but more steadfast. Because rebuilding means I'm not starting over, I'm starting *from experience.*

Your Reflection Moment

Question 1:
What area of your life have you been trying to
recover that God might be calling you to rebuild
instead?

Question 2:
What would rebuilding look like if you stopped
grieving what was and started embracing what
could be?

Action Step:
Write down three things you've lost, big or small.
Next to each one, write a single way you can
rebuild from it. Then pray this: "God, help me
release my need to recover what's gone, and teach
me to rebuild what's next. Give me the courage to
start, and the faith to finish."

That's where power returns: not in recovery, but in
resurrection through rebuilding.

Key Takeaway:

You can't recover what God called you to rebuild.
Some things weren't meant to be repaired; they
were meant to be reimagined. Rebuilding doesn't
erase the loss; it redeems it. It takes the lessons, not
the leftovers, and shapes them into something
stronger.

"When God Tells You to Loosen the Oars"

In leadership, we are taught to steer, to plan, to control every direction of the voyage. We map our routes, chart our timelines, and measure our success by how fast we move. But the truth is, there comes a time when God asks you to *drift.*

Drifting doesn't mean you're lost; it means you've surrendered control to the One who knows the currents better than you do. It's the moment when faith replaces force, when you stop fighting to prove you're still in charge and start trusting that grace will carry you where effort cannot.

Some leaders fear the drift because it feels like doing nothing. But spiritually, drifting is one of the most powerful forms of movement. It's rest wrapped in trust. It's the season where direction comes not from your strength, but from His sovereignty.

The Titanic teaches us that sometimes the pursuit of control leads to collision. The ship was so obsessed with direction that it forgot the ocean doesn't answer to human timelines. Likewise, when leaders push beyond divine pacing, they risk breaking what was meant to simply breathe.

Drifting is not about quitting: it's about *aligning.* It's knowing when to loosen your grip and let the Spirit adjust your course. It's learning to sit in the in-between seasons, when God says, *"Not yet,"* but your ambition screams, *"Now."*

The hardest part of drifting is not the stillness, it's the surrender. But it's in that sacred surrender that you discover your strength was never in the rowing; it was in the resting. Because only those who trust the current truly understand that even when you're not steering, you're still being carried.

Captain's Note

There were seasons I thought stillness meant I was falling behind. I equated silence with stagnation and pause with punishment. But I've learned that drifting under divine direction isn't delay, it's design.

When God tells you to loosen the oars, it's because He's aligning the wind. He's clearing unseen paths, preparing unseen doors, and testing whether your faith can float without friction. Drifting teaches discipline: the discipline to wait, to rest, and to let peace lead when pressure rises.

Sometimes the storm doesn't pass until you stop rowing. And sometimes, the blessing doesn't appear until you stop forcing it.

Reflection

- Where in my life am I still rowing when God is asking me to drift?
- What emotions arise when I'm not in control: fear, frustration, or faith?
- How has striving hindered my ability to hear divine direction?
- What would it look like to rest without retreating; to drift with purpose instead of panic?

Key Takeaway:

Drifting isn't drifting away; it's drifting into alignment. *It's the art of letting go without losing focus, of surrendering without sinking. When you learn how to drift, you stop fighting the waves and start trusting the wind. Because faith doesn't always require movement, sometimes it just requires* stillness that floats. ⚓

"Walking Into What's Next with Grace"

There comes a moment after the storm when the wind finally quiets, but your soul still remembers the sound of it. That's when grace steps in.

Grace teaches you how to move again without rushing. It teaches you to walk forward, not from fear, but from faith. It whispers, *"You survived. Now let Me show you how to thrive."*

Walking into what's next with grace means understanding that your next season doesn't need your striving; it needs your surrender. You don't have to prove you're ready for it; you just have to stay aligned with the One who prepared it.

There was a time when I thought forward motion meant force. If it wasn't happening fast, I assumed something was wrong. But I've learned that divine timing doesn't need defending. When grace leads, there's no rush, just rhythm.

The Titanic reminds us that haste without humility leads to heartbreak. They moved full speed, ignoring warning after warning, trying to prove what was already presumed: "unsinkable." But grace doesn't move to prove; it moves to *preserve.* It listens. It slows down. It honors process over pressure. As leaders, we often want to leap into the next thing, but grace invites us to *walk.*

To step gently. To move intentionally. To let peace, not pride, determine the pace.

You can tell when grace is guiding you; it doesn't feel forced. Doors open smoothly. Conversations align naturally. And instead of striving, you start flowing. That's not weakness; that's wisdom. That's the art of walking with God, not ahead of Him.

Leadership isn't just about having vision; it's about knowing how to transition. You can't carry old energy into a new assignment. If you rush what God is still revealing, you risk mismanaging the very thing He's maturing.

Walking into what's next with grace means:

- Leaving behind what no longer aligns, without resentment.
- Carrying lessons forward, without carrying baggage.
- Trusting the new season, even if you don't fully understand it yet.

Grace is both the guide and the guardrail. It slows you when ego tries to speed you. It strengthens you when doubt tries to stop you. And it steadies you when uncertainty tries to shake you.

There was a time I walked into every new thing wounded, still defending myself from old battles. But grace taught me how to enter healed, not hardened. It taught me that closure isn't revenge, it's peace. It's saying, *"I can bless what broke me and still move forward with dignity."*

You don't have to drag your past into your next season. You just have to walk differently; lighter, wiser, freer. The same God who carried you through the storm will guide you through the sunrise. He doesn't just rebuild; He repositions. He doesn't just restore; He *redeems.* So walk softly. Walk surely. Walk gracefully. Because the same wind that once tested you will now carry you.

Captain's Note

When I look back over every chapter of my life: the successes, the shifts, the heartbreaks, I can see God's hand in every transition. There were seasons where I tried to drag the old me into a new mission. But every time I did, He gently reminded me: "You can't enter what's next wearing yesterday's identity."

That's the power of grace. It doesn't erase what was; it *elevates* who you've become because of it. Grace allows you to walk into rooms without resentment, to speak without fear, and to lead without losing yourself. When grace guides you, your steps may be smaller, but they're surer. And even if you don't know where the path leads, you'll know Who's leading you.

Your Reflection Moment

Question 1:
What part of your old season are you still carrying into your new one?

Question 2:
Where might God be asking you to slow down and let grace, not urgency, lead the way?

Action Step:
Take a few quiet minutes this week and visualize your next season. See yourself walking into it with calm confidence.
Pray this: "God, teach me to walk into what's next with grace. Help me to release my need to rush and trust Your pace instead. Let my presence in this new place reflect peace, not pressure."

Write down how you want to *feel* in your next chapter — not what you want to accomplish.
Then lead from that posture.

Key Takeaway:

Grace is how you enter what's next without losing the peace you fought for. Move gently. Move wisely. Move with God, not ahead of Him.

Captain's Chapter Reflection: The Rebuilt Blueprint

Building Again: Stronger, Wiser, Anchored in Faith

What fell apart wasn't failure; it was a foundation check. Rebuilding isn't about returning to what was; it's about constructing what's meant to last. God doesn't waste wreckage; He repurposes it into revelation. This reflection is your moment to acknowledge what survived, what strengthened, and what still stands ready for the next voyage.

Reflection Prompts

1. **What have I learned about myself through the rebuilding process?**
2. **What pieces of the old blueprint no longer fit this season of leadership?**
3. **How can I honor the lessons from the wreckage without carrying the weight of it?**
4. **Where do I see evidence of God's restoration in my life or vision?**
5. **What am I building now that reflects not just experience, but divine wisdom?**

Captain's Notes

(Use this space to write freely.)

_____

_____

_____

_____

_____

_____

_____

_____

_____

_____

_____

_____

_____

_____

_____

_____

_____

_____

_____

_____

_____

_____

"You can't rebuild the same — you were never meant to. The storm didn't erase your calling; it refined your construction."
— *Jacqueline Boatwright-Daus*

EPILOGUE: SAILING INTO THE NEXT SEASON

"The Storm Didn't End Your Story"

Reflection

Every great voyage changes the captain. This book has been your voyage: through leadership storms, divine release, rebuilding seasons, and renewed faith. You've walked through moments that broke you and rebuilt you. You've learned that true leadership isn't about control; it's about *clarity*. It's about hearing God in the quiet and trusting Him in the chaos.

If you've made it here, you've survived your own Titanic. Maybe not an ocean, but a season, a loss, a betrayal, or a breaking point. Yet here you stand, stronger, wiser, and anchored deeper than before.

You now understand that storms don't sink purpose; they *shape* it. The water that threatened to drown you became the same water that washed away everything that wasn't meant to stay.

The Titanic sank because overconfidence silenced caution. But your ship stands because humility birthed wisdom.

Leadership Summation

Through these pages, you've uncovered what every great leader must learn:
 Understanding the Assignment revealed your purpose.
 Releasing the Lots taught you peace through letting go.
 Restoring Structure taught you order through obedience.
 Strategy After the Purge gave you direction through discernment.
Blueprints and Boundaries gave you strength through stewardship.
Moving Forward with Clarity gave you focus through faith.

This journey has shown you that God doesn't bless chaos. He blesses structure, order, and stewardship. He honors the leader who listens more than the one who leads loudest.

You've learned to rebuild with precision, not panic, and to understand that every setback was not the end of the vision, but the start of alignment.

Captain's Final Note

If I could look you in the eye, leader to leader, I'd tell you this: Don't apologize for outgrowing what was small. Don't stay where peace has left. Don't slow down your purpose to match someone else's pace.

You've earned this moment of clarity. You've earned the right to rebuild with wisdom. And you've earned the grace to move forward without guilt. Because now, you understand what it means to be anchored. Not in people. Not in pride, but in purpose.

The storms refined you, not ruined you. The separation saved you, not scarred you. And the lessons… those will guide you for a lifetime.

Lift your head, Captain. Adjust your sails. And lead again, with vision, with courage, and with clarity.

Final Takeaway

You are not the same person who started this voyage. You are wiser, calmer, stronger, and grounded in purpose. The ship may have tilted, but the music still played — and now, it's your turn to lead the next voyage with grace.

Closing Dedication

To every visionary who had to rebuild after the storm, to every leader who had to release what they loved to save what was divine —this is your reminder that God wastes nothing.

Every lesson was alignment. Every loss was preparation. And every comeback is proof that *purpose floats — even after the fall.*

Keep leading. Keep believing.
And as you rise, always —

Stay Juanderful.

TITANIC LEADERSHIP
10 Lessons from the Ship That Was Too Great to Fail

1 — The Titanic Effect

"The ship didn't fail because of one storm — it failed because everyone stopped paying attention."

The Titanic Effect is what happens when confidence turns into carelessness. It's the slow drift from awareness to assumption; the moment leaders stop checking the details because everything *looks* successful. The ship didn't sink from one storm or one bad decision; it sank because pride muted caution.

In leadership, the same thing happens when we start believing we're "unsinkable." We stop listening to warnings, we ignore small cracks, and we substitute busyness for vigilance.

The Titanic Effect is a warning against the comfort that comes with success; the temptation to relax when we should refine. Great leaders stay alert in calm waters. They double-check what's working, revisit what's drifting, and keep humility at the helm. Because what sinks ships isn't always the storm — sometimes it's the silence of those who stopped paying attention.

2 — Overworked or Over-Lifed

"Not every tired employee is overworked. Some are just over-lifed."

Every ship has a weight limit, not just in cargo, but in *capacity*. And while businesses don't sail on water, they can still sink under pressure.

In today's workplace, one of the heaviest burdens leaders face isn't lack of talent or resources; it's the growing number of over-lifed employees: individuals whose personal challenges spill into their professional performance. The result? A ship that's technically moving but slowly taking on water.

3 — Leadership Accountability vs. Responsibility

"You can't calm every storm, but you can build lifeboats strong enough to survive it."

When the Titanic sank, people blamed the captain, and rightly so, to a point. But the truth is, the ship didn't go down because of one man. It sank because of a combination of arrogance, system failure, and human limitation.

The same principle applies in today's workplace: leaders steer the ship, but they can't carry every passenger's personal baggage. Leadership bears accountability, not ownership, of the human experience on board.

4 — When the Captain Carries It All

"Even the strongest captain can't steer a ship that's carrying everyone's storm."

Leadership Feels the Strain First

As the emotional weight builds, it doesn't distribute evenly; it tilts upward. Leaders become the emotional container for everyone else's stress. Decision fatigue, compassion burnout, and constant crisis management start to feel "normal." But here's the truth: if the captain is too busy bailing water to steer, the whole ship is already off course.

5 — How Over-Lifed Employees Impact the Ship

"Ships don't sink because of the water around them — they sink when too much gets inside."

The Hidden Weight of Everyday Life

On the Titanic, not everyone carried luggage the same way. Some had trunks of luxury. Others carried everything they owned. Similarly, in business, employees bring different kinds of "baggage" aboard: financial stress, caregiving duties, health issues, emotional fatigue, or loss of motivation. When life feels heavy, work can't help but feel heavier.
The danger comes when leadership doesn't recognize that the ship's load isn't just professional, it's personal, too.

6 — The Cost of Misguided Decisions

"The Titanic didn't sink because it wasn't built well; it sank because those in command ignored clear warnings."

Watch For the Warning Signs

The cost of misguided decisions is rarely immediate; it's discovered in the aftermath, when leaders realize they were steering by pride instead of purpose. True strategy isn't about speed; it's about sensitivity; knowing when to move and when to pause. One wrong decision at the wrong time can shift the entire course of destiny.

7 — The Titanic Still Underwater

"Once considered unsinkable — now it can't even be raised."

The Legacy of Ignored Lessons

The Titanic is still sitting at the bottom of the ocean. Once hailed as *unsinkable,* now it's *unrecoverable.* That's not just a historical fact; it's a leadership warning. How many companies, teams, and visions have gone the same way? Once unstoppable. Now unrecognizable. Not because of one disaster but because no one had the humility to believe disaster was possible.

8 — The Lifeboat Principle

"You can't build lifeboats during the collision —
they must exist before the impact."

Leadership maturity means preparing before the crisis, not reacting to it. The Titanic wasn't doomed by one mistake; it was crippled by unpreparedness, a belief that nothing could go wrong. Many leaders make the same mistake: they wait for disaster to build structure.

The *Lifeboat Principle* reminds us that systems of support: faith, strategy, trusted counsel, prayer, and self-discipline, must be established long before the ship ever shakes. You can't construct emotional stability in the middle of heartbreak, nor can you develop faith in the middle of panic.

Lifeboats represent foresight; the wisdom to prepare for safety before you need saving. Every leader should build their lifeboats in seasons of peace: mentors who speak truth, habits that sustain health, prayer that anchors faith, and a team strong enough to row when waves rise. Because once impact hits, it's too late to start building what you should have already secured.

9 — The Music Still Played

"Even when the ship tilts, great leaders
keep the music playing, not to distract, but
to keep hope alive."

That's what great leaders do. They lead with calm when everyone else trembles. They remind others that even in crisis, beauty still exists. Leadership isn't always about fixing the problem; sometimes it's about holding the atmosphere. When panic rises, peace becomes your power. When people lose direction, your composure becomes the compass

10 — The Rebuild: Lessons Above the Surface

> *"Sometimes you can't recover, but you can always rebuild."*

Don't Raise the Wreck — Redesign the Ship

When you try to "recover," you're clinging to the past. When you rebuild, you're creating the future. The new Titanic museums, documentaries, and memorials don't glorify the ship; they honor the *growth* that came after it.

In business, rebuilding means:

- Changing what didn't work.
- Leading differently.
- Valuing people over performance.
- Learning before launching again

> *"Until our next sailing, Captain."*
> Jacqueline Boatwright-Daus

About the Author

Jacqueline Boatwright-Daus, BS, MBA, Ed.S. is a visionary entrepreneur, Certified Trichologist, and the dynamic founder of **Juanderful Enterprises LLC**, a diverse business ecosystem that unites beauty, leadership, education, and empowerment under one mission — to help others rise through faith, focus, and strategy.

Her story is not one of perfection, but of perseverance. Through seasons of both triumph and trial, Jacqueline discovered that leadership is less about position and more about purpose. She believes that God doesn't call the qualified — He qualifies the called. Her career, spanning multiple industries, is a living testimony of what happens when faith fuels focus and vision meets divine order.

With a Bachelor of Science in Pre-Law, a Master of Business Administration (MBA), and an Education Specialist (Ed.S.) degree in Educational Leadership, Jacqueline merges academic excellence with spiritual insight. Her experience ranges from corporate development and educational leadership to medical aesthetics, trichology, and entrepreneurship — making her a rare blend of strategy and spirit.

As the founder of Juanderful Aesthetics, a leading medical aesthetics and trichology clinic, she serves clients with both compassion and clinical precision. Her Juanderful Products line extends that same care through luxury, science-based hair and skincare solutions, designed to restore confidence, health, and radiance from the inside out. Through Jacqueleen's Southern Porch, her fine dining and hospitality brand, she redefines Southern comfort with elegance and grace — building businesses that serve both the body and the soul.

Beyond her ventures, Jacqueline is a teacher at heart. Through her Juanderful Leadership™ platform, she mentors visionaries, entrepreneurs, and professionals on how to navigate adversity, rebuild with resilience, and lead with unwavering faith. Her leadership philosophy is simple yet profound: "Faith is the anchor, strategy is the vessel, and leadership is the calling."

Jacqueline's journey has not been without storms — but she has learned that sometimes the waves that threaten to drown you are the same ones that carry you closer to your purpose. Her mission is to guide others in discovering that truth for themselves: that the storm doesn't come to destroy your foundation, but to reveal it.

She continues to inspire audiences across faith, business, and beauty industries through her writing, mentorship, and speaking engagements — empowering others to rise from the wreckage, rebuild with wisdom, and lead with grace.

When she isn't leading teams, developing products, or mentoring future leaders, Jacqueline enjoys quiet reflection, creative work, and family life alongside her husband, Kevin M. Daus, MD. Together, they embody the power of partnership, purpose, and unwavering faith — a living example of what it means to stay anchored in God's vision no matter how high the tides rise.